365

DAYS OF EMPOWERMENT

YOUR DAILY DOSE OF ENCOURAGEMENT

Copyright © 2024 by Minnina M. Smith

All rights reserved. No part of this publication may be reproduced, distributed, or transmitted in any form or by any means, including photocopying, recording, or other electronic or mechanical methods, without the prior written permission of the publisher, except in the case of brief quotations embodied in critical reviews and certain other noncommercial uses permitted by copyright law.

For permissions requests, write to the publisher, addressed "Attention: Permissions Coordinator," at the address below.

Minnina M. Smith
6941 N Trenholm Rd, Suite #F104, #362
Columbia, SC 29206

Email: minninasmith@thatdoseofencouragement.com

Published by Minnina M. Smith

Printed in the United States of America

First Printing: April 17, 2024

MINNINA M. SMITH

365

DAYS OF EMPOWERMENT

YOUR DAILY DOSE OF ENCOURAGEMENT

Embrace daily positivity, motivation, and encouragement with this uplifting companion book as you journey towards your divine purpose.

365 Days of Empowerment: Your Daily Dose of Encouragement is available via eBook and hardcopy.

Dedicated To:

My beloved parents, who may no longer walk this earth but remain eternally cherished for their loving upbringing. To my cherished siblings and friends, for their unwavering support. And to the divine presence of the Lord, whose guidance and protection have been my steadfast companions.

MINNINA M. SMITH
Introduction: Your Daily Companion to Strengthen and Encourage You

Welcome to "365 Days of Empowerment: Your Daily Dose of Encouragement"! In this book, you'll find a year-long journey filled with inspiration, motivation, and encouragement to uplift you through every day of the year. Life is a beautiful yet unpredictable journey, and this book is here to be your trusted companion as you navigate its highs and lows.

Each day, you'll discover a powerful message crafted to uplift your spirit, ignite your passion, and empower you to overcome any obstacles that come your way. Whether you're facing challenges, pursuing your purpose, experiencing love, joy, or sadness, this book is designed to provide you with the strength and encouragement you need to keep moving forward.

Life can be tough sometimes, and we all need a little extra support along the way. That's where "365 Days of Empowerment" comes in. Think of this book as your personal cheerleader, cheering you on as you tackle each day with courage and determination. It's filled with those little reminders that we all need from time to time—reminders that you are capable, worthy, and deserving of all the good things life has to offer.

Each daily entry is a gentle nudge to remind you that no matter what challenges you face, you have the inner strength and resilience to overcome them. Whether you're striving towards your goals, dealing with setbacks, or simply navigating the ups and downs of daily life, this book will be there to remind you that you are not alone.

In today's fast-paced world, it's easy to feel overwhelmed and discouraged. That's why it's so important to surround yourself with positivity and inspiration, and that's exactly what "365 Days of Empowerment" aims to provide. With its uplifting messages and words of encouragement, this book will help you stay focused, motivated, and inspired to live your best life.

So, as you embark on this journey through the pages of "365 Days of Empowerment," remember that you are not just reading a book—you are embarking on a transformative journey towards greater self-awareness, confidence, and empowerment. Allow yourself to be open to the messages and lessons that each day brings, and trust that they will guide you towards a brighter, more fulfilling future.

As you journey through the pages of this book day by day, may your faith be fortified or discovered, may you embrace the essence of faith. Let it serve as a constant reminder of your inner strength, resilience, and boundless potential. Take solace in the assurance that regardless of the hurdles ahead, you possess the innate ability to conquer them. Above all, never forget that you are cherished, esteemed, and deserving of life's abundant blessings.

Here's to a year filled with empowerment, growth, and endless possibilities. Let's embark on this journey together, one day at a time. You've got this, let's go!

-Minnina M. Smith

MINNINA M. SMITH

TABLE OF CONTENTS

Dedicated To	5
Introduction: Your Daily Companion to Strengthen and Encourage You	6
January	12
Inspiration for Setting Goals and Vision Planning	12
February	44
Self-Love and Care	44
March	74
Mindful Eating and Nutrition	74
April	106
Embracing Change and Growth	106
May	137
Cultivating Gratitude and Positivity	137
June	169
Finding Balance and Harmony	169
July	200
Stress Management and Resilience	200
August	232

Fitness and Exercise Goals	232
September	264
Self-Mental Health Awareness	264
October	296
Overcoming Fear and Limiting Beliefs	296
November	328
Building Healthy Relationships	328
December	359
Reflection And Renewal During The Last Month Of The Year	359

January

—

Inspiration for Setting Goals and Vision Planning

January 1

Embracing New Beginnings

Embracing new beginnings means stepping into the unknown with courage and faith. It's about letting go of the past and embracing the possibilities of the future. Remember, every sunrise brings a fresh start, a chance to rewrite your story and pursue your purpose. It's okay to feel a little scared or uncertain—it's all part of the journey.

Trust in yourself and in God, knowing that you have the strength and resilience to navigate whatever comes your way. Embrace the beauty of new beginnings, and watch as they unfold into moments of growth, joy, and endless possibilities.

January 2

Setting Intentions for the Year Ahead

As we embark on a new year, setting intentions paves the path for our journey ahead. It's about aligning our desires with our actions, nurturing our purpose, and embracing the power of intentionality. Whether it's pursuing personal growth, cultivating joy, or walking out our purpose, intentions give us direction and insight.

So, take a moment to reflect on what truly matters to you, what ignites your soul, and what you wish to create in the coming year. With clear intentions and unwavering commitment, you have the power to shape your reality and create a life filled with meaning, fulfillment, and abundance.

January 3

Trusting in Divine Guidance

Trusting in Divine Guidance is like navigating through a dark tunnel with the assurance that there's light at the end. It's about surrendering control, knowing that there's a higher power orchestrating the universe's symphony. Sometimes, life throws us curveballs, but amidst the chaos, faith whispers, "Trust the journey."

It's in those moments of uncertainty that we lean on our spiritual compass, allowing it to guide us towards our true purpose. Remember, even in the midst of storms, the stars still shine. So, hold steadfast to your faith, for divine guidance leads to unexpected blessings and miraculous transformations. Trust, and you'll find your way.

January 4

Overcoming Self-Doubt

In the journey of life, self-doubt often sneaks in, whispering lies about our abilities and worth. But just like a tiny seed can grow into a mighty tree, your faith in yourself can overcome any doubt. As Philippians 4:13 assures, "I can do all things through Christ who strengthens me."

Trust in your inner strength, embrace your uniqueness, and step boldly into your purpose. Remember, even the strongest storms eventually pass, and you emerge stronger. So, silence the doubt, believe in yourself, and watch as you soar to heights you never imagined possible.

January 5

Cultivating Gratitude

In the garden of life, gratitude is the water that nourishes our soul, allowing us to bloom amidst life's challenges. As Oprah Winfrey once said, 'Be thankful for what you have; you'll end up having more. If you concentrate on what you don't have, you will never, ever have enough.'

Let's cultivate gratitude like a gardener tends to their prized flowers— with care, consistency, and appreciation. Even in the midst of hardships, let's find something to be thankful for, for it is in gratitude that we find the true richness of life, abundance, and joy.

January 6

Finding Strength in Adversity

Hey there, friend! Life throws us curveballs, right? But guess what? You're stronger than you think. When it gets hard, remember, you've got what it takes to overcome any obstacle that comes your way. It's like that verse says, "When you go through deep waters, I will be with you" (Isaiah 43:2).

So, don't sweat the small stuff. You've got a whole squad cheering you on—God's got your back, and so do I. Keep your chin up, keep pushing forward, and watch as you emerge from adversity even stronger than before. You've got this!

January 7

Pursuing Passion Versus Pursuing Purpose

Ever find yourself torn between chasing your passions or following your purpose? It's like deciding between pizza and tacos—both are awesome, but which one satisfies your soul? Let me tell you, I've been there! Pursuing passion feels like fireworks in your heart, but purpose? It's like finding your missing puzzle piece. Trust me, I get the struggle.

But here's the thing: when passion meets purpose, magic happens. So, embrace your passions, follow your purpose, and watch as your life unfolds into something truly extraordinary. You've got this, and I'm cheering you on every step of the way!

January 8

Navigating Challenges with Faith

Life's like a rollercoaster, full of twists and turns, right? But here's the thing: with a dash of faith, you can ride it like a pro! As Martin Luther King Jr. said, "Faith is taking the first step even when you don't see the whole staircase."

Trusting in God's plan, like one of my favorite scriptures, Psalm 23:4 reminds us, "Even though I walk through the valley of the shadow of death, I will fear no evil, for you are with me," keeps us steady through the storms. So buckle up, keep that faith alive, and let's tackle those challenges head-on! You've got this!

January 9

Embracing Your Authenticity

Today's message is all about embracing your authenticity. You know, the silly, unique, totally-you parts that make you, well, YOU! So, let go of trying to fit into someone else's mold and rock what makes you special.

Whether you're a little loud, a tad introverted, or somewhere in between, own it! Because when you embrace your divine authenticity, you give others permission to do the same. So, let your uniquely made self-flag fly, shine your light bright, and remember, there's nobody else out there quite like you—and that's the power you possess, so own it!

January 10

Letting Go of Fear

Hello there! Let's talk about something we all deal with: fear. Yep, that sneaky little voice in our heads that tells us we're not good enough, smart enough, or brave enough. But guess what? You are! So, here's a little reminder from Psalms 56:3: "When I am afraid, I put my trust in you."

Trust in the Lord above and in yourself. Now, how do we kick fear to the curb? Well, first, acknowledge it. Yep, give it a little nod and then tell it to take a hike. Next, focus on the present moment. Take a deep breath and remind yourself that you've got this. And finally, take action! Face your fears head-on and watch them shrink away. You're stronger than you think, friend. So go out there and show fear who's boss!

January 11

Honoring Your Inner Voice

Hello, beautiful soul! Today's message is all about honoring your inner voice. You know that little voice inside of you that nudges you in the right direction? Yeah, that's your intuition, your gut feeling, and it's there for a reason. Trust it!

God has given us this amazing gift of wisdom, and when we listen to that inner voice, we're tapping into His divine guidance. So, take a moment today to quiet the noise around you, listen to that gentle whisper within, and follow where it leads. You've got this, and remember, God's got your back every step of the way!

January 12

Restoring Hope

Restoring hope isn't just about putting a smile on your face; it's about mending the broken pieces of your heart and rediscovering the light within. It's those moments when life knocks you down, and you find the strength to get back up again, even if your knees are trembling.

It's about believing in tomorrow, even when today feels like a storm. So, if you're feeling lost or beaten down, remember this: hope isn't lost—it's just waiting for you to embrace it. So, let's dust off those goals & divine given dreams, wipe away the tears, and walk hand in hand towards a brighter tomorrow.

January 13

Celebrating Small Wins

Have you ever felt like life's just one big hurdle after another? I've been there too. But guess what? It's those small wins that keep us going! Whether it's finally finishing that project you've been putting off or just getting out of bed on a tough day, every little victory counts. So, let's celebrate them!

Remember, it's not always about the big milestones—it's the little moments of progress that truly add up. Keep pushing forward, keep celebrating those wins, and most importantly, keep being awesome!

January 14

Fostering Healthy Relationships

Building strong relationships isn't just about finding the perfect match—it's about nurturing connections with the people who bring out the best in us. From family bonds to friendships and everything in between, it's those heart-to-heart conversations, shared laughs, and moments of vulnerability that truly strengthen our bonds.

Sure, there'll be ups and downs, disagreements, and misunderstandings along the way, but that's all part of the journey. So, let's lean into those connections, communicate openly, and show up for each other—because at the end of the day, it's the people in our lives who make it all worth it.

January 15

Trusting the Timing of Your Life

In life, we often find ourselves racing against the clock, impatiently waiting for things to fall into place. But here's the thing: God's timing is always perfect, even when it doesn't align with our own. Trusting in His plan can be challenging, especially when we're eager for answers or struggling with uncertainty.

But remember, every delay, setback, or closed door is simply a detour guiding us towards something greater. So, take a deep breath, surrender control, and trust that everything will unfold exactly as it's meant to. Your journey may have its twists and turns, but His timing is always worth the wait.

January 16

Finding Joy in the Journey

As we journey through life, it's easy to get caught up in the hustle and bustle, isn't it? But you know what? There's so much beauty to be found in the little moments—the laughter of loved ones, the warmth of the sun on your face, and the peace that comes from knowing you're exactly where you're meant to be.

I've learned that joy isn't just about the big moments or achievements; it's about finding contentment and gratitude in everyday life. It's about trusting in God's plan for your life and knowing that even in the tough times, there's always something to be thankful for. So, here's to finding joy in the journey—embracing each day with an open heart, a grateful spirit, and a whole lot of faith. Remember, no matter what comes your way, you're never alone. God is with you every step of the way, guiding you, supporting you, and filling your heart with joy.

January 17

Forgiving Yourself and Others

As you flip through these pages, let me share a little secret with you: forgiveness isn't just about letting go of the past; it's about freeing yourself from its grip. Trust me, I've been there. I know how hard it can be to forgive yourself for past mistakes or to forgive others who've wronged you.

But here's the thing: when you hold onto resentment, you're only hurting yourself. So, let's take a journey together—a journey of grace, mercy, and redemption. Let's learn to forgive ourselves and others, just as our faith teaches us. It's time to set ourselves free.

January 18

Cultivating a Positive Mindset

Coming from a negative mindset can feel like being stuck in a dark tunnel with no way out. Trust me, I've been there. When I lost my mother at 16, I thought my world was over. But did I stay in that gloomy place? Heck no! I fought tooth and nail to break free and even found God along the way (though He wasn't lost, lol it was I that was lost). And you know what?

It wasn't easy but I can humbly but proudly say, look at me now! A college grad, a military vet, a business owner, a homeowner, an author, a certified life and health coach—yes, I wear many hats! And you know what? God's got more in store for not just me, but for you too, once you choose to embrace that positive mindset. Let's go, you got this!

January 19

Shedding the Weight of Negativity

Surrounding yourself with negative energy can impact your outlook and well-being. Whether you're the one spreading negativity or absorbing it from others, it's crucial to recognize its effects. There is a proverb that says, "Walk with the wise and become wise, for a companion of fools suffers harm" (Proverbs 13:20).

Just as bad company corrupts good character, negative influences can drain your positivity. Empower your surroundings with positivity, seeking companionship that uplifts and aligns with your life's purpose.

January 20

Strengthening Your Faith Foundation

In life, we often face uncertainties that challenge our faith foundation. But amidst the chaos, we find strength. Faith isn't just about blind belief; it's about trust, conviction, and perseverance. It's the unwavering confidence that guides us through the darkest nights and celebrates our brightest days. As Hebrews 11:1 says, "Now faith is confidence in what we hope for and assurance about what we do not see."

Faith originates from the depths of our souls, anchoring us in hope and empowering us to embrace the unknown with courage and resilience. Let your faith be your rock, your anchor, and your guiding light.

January 21

Practicing Self-Compassion

In a world where perfection seems like the ultimate goal, practicing self-compassion can feel like a radical act of rebellion. It's about embracing your flaws, your quirks, and your imperfections with kindness and understanding.

I've learned that it's okay to stumble, to make mistakes, and to not have it all together all the time. Self-compassion is about treating yourself with the same love and care that you would offer to a friend in need. It's about acknowledging your humanity, embracing your worthiness, and giving yourself permission to be perfectly imperfect.

January 22

Time To Step Out of Your Comfort Zone

It's time to shake things up! We all have that thing looming over us, making our palms sweaty and hearts race. But guess what? It's time to tackle it head-on! Whether it's going live on social media, teaching that class, changing careers, or even just striking up a conversation with a stranger, let's challenge ourselves to step out of our cozy comfort zones.

Sure, it might be nerve-wracking at first, but trust me, amazing things lie beyond that fear. Who knows? You might just uncover hidden talents, make new connections, or discover a whole new world of possibilities. So, what are you waiting for? Go and be great!

January 23

Embracing the Power of Prayer

Hey there, friend. When's the last time you prayed? It's okay if it's been a while or if you've never felt quite comfortable with it. Let me share a little secret with you: prayer is simply communication with God. It's pouring out your heart, sharing your hopes, fears, and dreams with the One who loves you unconditionally.

In times of trouble, we're encouraged to pray. Are you familiar with the story of Hannah, who prayed earnestly for a child? Or King David, who poured out his heart in the Psalms? Their prayers were answered, and so can yours.

So, what can you pray for? Anything and everything! Seek God's guidance, peace, and provision. And know this: He hears you. "Call to me and I will answer you" (Jeremiah 33:3). So go ahead, pour out your heart to Him. He's listening.

January 24

Creating a Vision for Your Future

I don't know about you, but I love a good vision board and journal! There's something wonderful about mapping out dreams and pouring your heart onto paper. Listen, Habakkuk tells us, "Write the vision and make it plain on tablets, that he may run who reads it." So, let's get to work!

Let's dream big, set goals, and take action. As we craft our vision for the future, let's also trust in the divine plan and believe that every step forward brings us closer to our destiny. Your dreams are valid, your journey is significant—let's make them a reality!

January 25

Living with Purpose and Intention

Life is for living, every moment with purpose. Uncover your reason for being, live with intentionality. Embrace each day passionately, pursuing your purpose and spreading love and joy.

Amidst the grind, remember to have fun. Dance, laugh, cherish life's beauty. Find fulfillment in every step, leaving a legacy of love and inspiration. Live with purpose, intention, and to the fullest.

January 26

Exploring the Benefits of Mindfulness and Alone Time

Let's talk about something really important—taking some time for yourself. You know that alone time where you can just be with your thoughts and feelings without any distractions. It might seem unexpected in today's busy world, but trust me, it's absolutely crucial. When you give yourself the gift of mindfulness and solitude, you're actually nurturing your mental and emotional well-being.

Think of it as a recharge for your soul. It's a chance to slow down, breathe, and connect with yourself on a deeper level. You'll find clarity, peace, and a renewed sense of perspective. So, next time you're feeling overwhelmed or stressed, remember the power of mindfulness and alone time. It's not selfish—it's self-care, and you deserve it.

January 27

You Are Stronger Than You Think

Today, remind yourself of your inner strength. You've faced challenges in the past and emerged victorious. Trust in your resilience; you have the power to overcome any obstacle that crosses your path. Embrace confidence in yourself and your capabilities. With determination and belief, you can conquer whatever challenges lie ahead.

You possess untapped potential and unwavering courage within you. Take a moment to acknowledge your past victories and draw strength from them. Believe in your ability to navigate through today's trials and emerge stronger on the other side. You are resilient, capable, and destined for greatness.

January 28

Gratitude for Uplifters: Honoring Those Who Support You

In our journey through life, it's vital to acknowledge and cherish those who infuse our days with positivity. Take a moment to express gratitude for the individuals who uplift and support you, for their presence is a beacon of light amidst life's challenges.

Surrounding yourself with such souls fosters an environment of encouragement and growth. Together, united in kindness and support, we possess the power to create a brighter tomorrow. Embrace the joy of camaraderie, for in fostering meaningful connections, we cultivate a world brimming with hope, resilience, and boundless possibilities.

January 29

Waking Up with Purpose In Mind

Every morning presents an opportunity to awaken with intention. Set clear intentions for your day, directing your actions towards your goals and aspirations. Each moment holds significance; commit to infusing it with purpose and meaning.

Whether it's a small task or a significant decision, approach it intentionally. Your actions, no matter how seemingly insignificant, possess the power to shape your reality. By embracing purposeful living, you take control of your destiny, steering it towards fulfillment and success. So, as you rise each morning, remember the power you hold to shape your life's narrative through purposeful action.

January 30

Journey Reflection: Celebrating Growth and Resilience

Reflecting on your journey, take pride in how far you've come. Each step forward, no matter how small, speaks volumes about your strength and resilience. Celebrate your growth and achievements, acknowledging the obstacles you've overcome and the challenges you've conquered.

Remember the moments of doubt and fear you've faced, and recognize the courage it took to persevere. Every experience has shaped you into the person you are today. Embrace your progress, and hold onto the belief that you are capable of even greater things. Your journey is a testament to your unwavering determination and inner strength.

January 31

Embrace New Beginnings Fearlessly

As this month draws to a close, let's reflect on the journey behind us and the path ahead. Remember, every ending marks the start of something new. It's a chance to turn the page, embrace fresh opportunities, and step forward with renewed optimism and courage.

Whatever challenges may come your way, approach them with a sense of resilience and determination. Believe in your ability to navigate the twists and turns of life's journey. Embrace the unknown with an open heart and a steadfast resolve. Your future is bright, filled with endless possibilities waiting to be discovered. Seize them with confidence and purpose.

February

—

Self-Love and Care

February 1

Soul Nourishment: Embracing Your Divine Design

Take a moment amidst life's rush to nourish your soul. Reflect on the truth that you are fearfully and wonderfully made. In the chaos, find solace in knowing that you are intricately crafted, with purpose woven into every fiber of your being.

Embrace your uniqueness, for you are a masterpiece of divine design. Let this knowledge be the foundation upon which you build your day. With each breath, remind yourself of your inherent worth and value. As you journey through today, carry this truth with you, allowing it to inspire and uplift you in all that you do.

February 2

Self-Care Isn't Selfish—It's Essential

Self-care isn't selfish—it's essential. In a world where we often prioritize the needs of others, it's vital to remember to nurture our own well-being. By treating ourselves with kindness and compassion, we replenish our spirits, recharge our energy, and foster inner strength.

Embrace moments of self-care as acts of love, acknowledging your worthiness and honoring your needs. When you prioritize self-care, you enhance your ability to show up fully for others and for yourself. Remember, you deserve the same level of care and attention that you so generously give to those around you. Take time for yourself, guilt-free.

February 3

Divine Whispers: Embracing God's Endless Love

In the serene stillness of life's pauses, heed the gentle murmurs of your heart. God's boundless love envelops you, transcending time, and space. Embrace the divine whispers that echo within, for they carry messages of hope, grace, and unfathomable affection.

Amidst the chaos of existence, find solace in the knowledge that you are deeply cherished and valued. Allow the quiet moments to serve as a sanctuary, where the love of the divine washes over you like a soothing balm. Open your heart to receive the abundance of love that God tirelessly pours upon you, for His love knows no bounds.

MINNINA M. SMITH
February 4

Cherish Your Individuality

As February unfolds, let's cherish our individuality, seeing beauty in our imperfections. Embrace your uniqueness, for it adds color to the world. Let's cultivate gratitude for our journey, embracing each flaw as a reminder of our humanity and a testament to our resilience.

February 5

Embrace Self-Kindness

In a world that often demands so much from us, it's crucial to remember the importance of treating yourself with kindness. Take a moment to pause and reflect on all that you've accomplished, big or small. You deserve love, respect, and compassion—not just from others, but from yourself too. Embrace your flaws and imperfections, for they make you beautifully human. Listen to your needs and honor them with gentle care.

Give yourself permission to rest, recharge, and prioritize your well-being. Remember, you are worthy of love and kindness, both from within and from the world around you.

February 6

Cultivating Inner Peace

Let's talk about finding that inner peace we all crave. It's about taking a moment to breathe, letting go of worries, and trusting that everything's gonna work out just fine. Whether you're praying, meditating, or just chilling out, find what brings you that calmness in your soul.

Remember, faith is like a steady anchor in the stormy seas of life. So, when things get crazy, lean into that faith, trust in the bigger picture, and let your worries float away. You got this! Keep cultivating that inner peace, and watch how it transforms your world.

February 7

Honoring Your Boundaries

So, let's talk about something super important: honoring your boundaries. It's easy to get caught up in saying yes to everything and everyone, but remember, it's totally okay to say no when something doesn't feel right or align with your values.

Your boundaries are like your personal bubble, and it's crucial to protect them. So, don't be afraid to speak up and let people know what you're comfortable with. You deserve to feel respected and valued, and setting boundaries is a big part of that.

February 8

Investing in Your Happiness

Here's a little secret, you deserve to be happy. Seriously, your happiness matters more than you know. So, don't forget to invest in it, whether that means doing things that make you smile, spending time with people who lift you up, or simply taking a moment to appreciate the little things in life.

You've got this, and you deserve all the happiness in the world. Keep doing what makes your heart sing, because you deserve nothing less.

February 9

Embracing Your Unique Journey

Quick question—how are you feeling about where you're at in life right now? Are you content with the path you're on, or are you craving something more?

Regardless of where you stand, I want you to know that your journey is uniquely yours. Embrace every twist, turn, and detour along the way, because each step is leading you somewhere meaningful.

So, whether you're basking in success or navigating uncertainty, remember that you're exactly where you need to be. Keep embracing your journey, and don't forget to enjoy the ride.

February 10

Celebrating Your Progress

If no one has told you allow me to say how proud I am of you! Seriously, the progress you've made should fill your heart with joy and gratitude.

You've been putting in the work, stepping out in faith, and trusting in God's plan for your life. And let me tell you, it's paying off! Each step forward, no matter how small, is worth celebrating.

So, take a moment to pat yourself on the back, give yourself a high five, or do a little happy dance—whatever feels right for you. You've come so far, and I can't wait to see where God takes you next. Keep going, keep shining bright and walking in faith. You've got this!

February 11

Listening to Your Heart's Desires

Ever stop to wonder what your heart truly craves? Maybe it's that trip you've been dreaming of or a career change you've been putting off. What's holding you back from pursuing those desires that ignite your soul? It's time to take a minute, tune in and listen.

February 12

Choose Joy Today

Just a friendly reminder for today: choose joy, no matter what comes your way. Don't let anyone or anything shift your mood. Embrace the little moments of happiness, laugh a little louder, and smile a little brighter.

Life's too short to dwell on the negatives, so focus on the positives and let your inner light shine. You deserve to feel joyful and content, so go ahead and spread those good vibes wherever you go. Remember, happiness is a choice, and today, I hope you choose joy.

February 13

Respecting Your Body and Mind

Just a gentle reminder for today: respect your body and mind like the precious gifts they are. Take a moment to nourish yourself with positive thoughts, healthy food, and a little bit of movement. You deserve to feel good inside and out.

Remember, your body is a temple, and your mind is a sanctuary. Treat them with love and care and watch how they flourish. Embrace the journey of self-discovery and self-acceptance. You're stronger than you think, take care of yourself.

February 14

Finding Comfort in Your Own Company

On Valentine's Day, remember this: whether you're single, taken, or somewhere in between, the most important relationship you'll ever have is with yourself. So, take some time to appreciate your own company. Treat yourself to something special, whether it's a cozy night in with your favorite movie or a solo adventure exploring your city.

Embrace the love that surrounds you from friends, family, and even pets. And most importantly, remember that you are worthy of love and happiness, no matter your relationship status. So go ahead, celebrate the love that exists within you, and know that you are cherished beyond measure.

February 15

Embracing Moments of Rest and Relaxation

Hey, you know when life gets crazy busy, and it feels like there's a million things on your plate? I have been there, done that! But you know what? In the midst of all that chaos, it's super important to carve out some time for yourself. Seriously, you must prioritize those moments of rest and relaxation.

Whether it's chilling with a good book, taking a long bath, or just lounging around doing absolutely nothing, make sure you give yourself that break you deserve. Trust me, it'll recharge your batteries and help you tackle whatever comes your way with a fresh perspective.

February 16

Recognizing Your Worthiness

You know, sometimes it's easy to forget just how worthy and valuable you truly are. But guess what? You are absolutely worth it—every bit of it. Remember the story of the prodigal son? Even when he strayed, his father welcomed him back with open arms, showing him just how loved and worthy he was.

That's how God sees you too. You're His beloved child, cherished and worthy in His eyes. So, don't let doubts or insecurities creep in. Stand tall, embrace your worthiness, and walk confidently in the knowledge that you are deeply loved and valued. Make sure you stay amazing!

February 17

Fueling Your Spirit

Feeling a bit down lately? Let's talk about fueling your spirit and lifting yourself up, even when life throws curveballs your way. Think about it like this: Remember that time when everything seemed to be going wrong, and you felt like you were stuck in a rut? I know, not a fun memory. But what did you do to pull yourself out of it? Maybe you turned to your faith, seeking comfort and guidance in prayer. Or perhaps you found solace in spending time with loved ones, soaking up their positive energy and support.

So here's the thing: when you're feeling low, it's crucial to fill your spirit with positivity and light (just like the light of the Lord that brightens up the darkest of nights). Whether it's through prayer, meditation, surrounding yourself with uplifting people, or simply doing something that brings you joy, find what works for you and make it a priority. Remember, you have the power to uplift yourself, even in the darkest of times. So go ahead, fuel your spirit with faith, love, and positivity.

February 18

Acknowledging Your Strengths

Listen up. It's time to give credit where it's due. You've got strengths, and it's about time you acknowledged them. Stop downplaying your abilities and start owning them like a boss. You're not just good at what you do, you're darn amazing.

So, next time you catch yourself doubting, take a deep breath and remind yourself of all the awesome things you bring to the table. Step up and own your strengths like the CEO of your own life. It's not arrogance; it's confidence. And trust me, the world needs more of that. So, stand tall, embrace your strengths, and let them shine bright like the diamonds they are.

February 19

Embracing Your Flaws as Beautiful Imperfections

Can we be real for a sec. We all have flaws, right? But here's the kicker: those flaws? They're what make us beautifully imperfect. I mean, seriously, show me someone without a single flaw, and I'll hand you a cool million dollars!

But until then, let's own those imperfections like the badges of honor they are. They're what make us unique, what give us character. So next time you're feeling down about that "flaw," remember, it's just a little quirk that makes you, well, you. And trust me, you're pretty darn awesome just the way you are!

February 20

Investing in Your Growth and Development

Investing in your growth and development isn't just about adding skills or knowledge—it's about nurturing your soul. It's about taking those little steps every day to become the best version of yourself. Maybe it's reading that book you've been eyeing, signing up for that class you've been curious about, or simply taking time for reflection and self-care.

Whatever it looks like for you, know that every effort you make towards your personal growth is an investment in your future. So keep going, keep learning, and keep evolving. The journey may be challenging at times, but the rewards are immeasurable.

February 21

Affirming Your Value and Importance

Today, let's take a moment to remind ourselves of something crucial—you are valuable and important. Yes, you! In a world that often tries to make us feel small or insignificant, it's essential to recognize our worth.

You bring something unique and irreplaceable to the table, whether it's your kindness, creativity, or simply your presence. Embrace your strengths, acknowledge your contributions, and never underestimate the impact you have on those around you. So, the next time doubt creeps in, remember: you matter, you are valued, and you are an essential part of this beautiful tapestry called life.

February 22

Giving Yourself Permission to Thrive

In this journey called life, it's easy to get caught up in the hustle and bustle, isn't it? But here's the thing—you deserve to thrive. Yes, you heard me right. It's not selfish or greedy to want more out of life. So, today, I want to remind you to give yourself permission to thrive.

Lean into your passions, chase your dreams, go after your divine purpose, and embrace every opportunity that comes your way. You have everything it takes to shine bright and make a difference in this world. So go ahead, step into your power, and let your light shine like never before.

February 23

Finding Balance in Your Life

Finding balance in life is like walking a tightrope—it's not always easy, but it's worth the effort. Sometimes, we're juggling so many things at once that we forget to take a step back and breathe. But amidst the chaos, it's crucial to find moments of stillness and peace.

Whether it's through meditation, a walk-in nature, or simply sitting quietly with your thoughts, carving out time for yourself is essential. Remember, you can't pour from an empty cup. So, take care of yourself, find balance amid life's craziness, and watch as everything falls into place.

February 24

Treasuring Your Journey of Self-Discovery

Oh, the word "self-discovery"! Do we tiptoe towards it or dive right in? It's like embarking on a treasure hunt, isn't it? Each step revealing something new and exciting about ourselves. So, let's embrace this journey with curiosity and excitement!

Peel back the layers, uncover the hidden gems within. It's not always about finding answers but relishing in the process. Celebrate every "aha" moment, every twist and turn. Remember, it's okay to stumble along the way; that's how we learn and grow. So, treasure this journey of self-discovery—it's your greatest adventure yet!

February 25

Showering Yourself with Grace and Forgiveness

It can be tough, I get it, to forgive yourself and move on from the past. But you know what? You deserve a little grace. Just like how God shows us endless grace every single day, even when we mess up.

Remember when Jesus forgave Peter after he denied Him three times? (Luke 22:61-62) That's the kind of love and forgiveness we're talking about here. So, take a deep breath, let go of that burden, and allow yourself to be showered with grace and forgiveness. You're worthy of it, my friend.

February 26

Believing in Your Self

Sometimes, it feels like you're on your own island with this big, bold vision swirling around in your head. But listen, you've got what it takes! Believe in yourself, even when the waves of doubt try to knock you down. Remember, every great journey starts with a single step.

Trust your instincts, follow your heart, and keep moving forward, one tiny victory at a time. You're stronger than you realize, and your purpose is worth pursuing. So, take a deep breath, hold onto hope, have faith and believe in the greatness that lies within you. You've got what it takes to shine!

February 27

Nourishing Your Mind, Body, and Soul

In nurturing our minds, bodies, and souls, we honor the divine gift bestowed upon us. For just as a garden thrives with balanced care—watering its roots, tending its soil, and basking in the sun—so too must we tend to our holistic well-being. As Psalm 23:3 reminds us, "He restores my soul. He leads me in paths of righteousness for his name's sake."

Through this sacred balance, we embark on a journey of restoration and fulfillment, embracing the interconnectedness of our being. Let us nourish ourselves wholly, guided by faith, to flourish in the abundant grace of our Creator.

February 28

Celebrating Black History: Embracing Love and Resilience

In honor of Black History Month, let's reflect on the incredible resilience and love demonstrated by black/African American individuals throughout history. Take a moment to ponder: How can I love others better? Consider the inspiring example of Harriet Tubman, who overcame immense challenges to lead others to freedom through the Underground Railroad.

Despite facing oppression and adversity, her unwavering love for humanity drove her to fight for justice and equality. Today, let's embody that same spirit of love and resilience in our own lives. Let's strive to love others with compassion, empathy, and courage, knowing that love has the power to transform lives and build a brighter, more inclusive future.

February 29

Leap Year Blessings: Embracing Divine Surprises
(If this month falls on a leap year guess what, you get a bonus day today!)

If this year falls on a leap year, consider it a gentle reminder of the unexpected blessings that grace our lives. Fun fact, leap years occur every four years to synchronize the calendar with the solar year. Just as an extra day is gifted to us, so too are countless opportunities for growth, love, and miracles. Reflect on the abundance surrounding you and marvel at the blessings you've received. How blessed are you to witness each dawn, to experience love's embrace, and to journey through life's adventures?

Embrace this extra day with gratitude, knowing that every moment is a precious gift from above. Leap forward with faith and embrace the divine surprises awaiting you.

March

—

Mindful Eating and Nutrition

March 1

The Importance of Mindful Eating

In the hustle and bustle of life, we often overlook the significance of mindful eating. Yet, this simple practice holds immense power. Mindful eating invites us to slow down, savor each bite, and truly connect with our food. It encourages us to listen to our bodies, honoring its hunger and fullness cues.

By being present in the moment, we cultivate a deeper appreciation for the nourishment our meals provide. Let us embrace mindful eating as a sacred act, one that nurtures our body, mind, and spirit. May it lead us to a place of greater health, gratitude, and inner peace.

March 2

Cultivating Gratitude for Nourishment

In the daily hustle of life, let's pause to cultivate gratitude for the nourishment we receive. Each meal, each morsel, is a gift—a testament to the abundance surrounding us. Let's savor the flavors, acknowledge the hands that brought it to our table, and honor the nutrients fueling our bodies.

Gratitude transforms the act of eating into a sacred ritual, a communion with the universe. As we nourish our bodies, let's also nourish our spirits with thankfulness. For in cultivating gratitude for nourishment, we cultivate an attitude of abundance and contentment that permeates every aspect of our lives.

March 3

Listening to Your Body's Hunger Cues

As you embark on your journey toward better health, remember to tune in to the whispers of your body. Pay attention to its hunger cues, subtle signals guiding you toward nourishment and balance. Whether it's a rumble in your stomach or a gentle pang of hunger, honor these cues with mindful awareness. Resist the urge to ignore or suppress them, for they are your body's way of communicating its needs.

By listening attentively and responding with kindness, you cultivate a deeper connection with yourself and foster a harmonious relationship with food. Trust in your body's wisdom—it knows what it needs to thrive.

Mach 4

Finding Joy in Cooking and Meal Preparation

In the rhythm of chopping vegetables and stirring pots, there lies a profound opportunity to discover joy in cooking and meal preparation. As you engage in this daily ritual, let it be more than a mere task but a sacred act of nourishment for body and soul. Embrace the vibrant colors, rich aromas, and wholesome ingredients that grace your kitchen.

Allow cooking to become a mindful practice, a moment of pause amidst life's hustle and bustle. With each dish you create, infuse it with love, intention, and gratitude. For in this simple act, you cultivate wellness from the inside out.

March 5

Exploring the Power of Whole Foods

As we delve into the profound impact of whole foods, let's marvel at their transformative power on our health journey. Whole foods, bursting with nutrients and vitality, nourish not only our bodies but our spirits as well. Each bite is a testament to the abundance of nature and the intricate dance of flavors and textures it offers.

Let us embrace the simplicity and purity of whole foods, recognizing them as the foundation of vibrant well-being. With each mindful choice, we affirm our commitment to honoring our bodies and nurturing our souls. Let the journey of exploring whole foods ignite a spark of vitality within us.

March 6

Embracing Balance in Your Diet

Embracing balance in your diet is not about restriction, but about nourishing your body and soul with intention. Seek harmony in your food choices, incorporating a variety of nutrient-rich foods that fuel your vitality. Listen to your body's cues, honoring both hunger and fullness with mindfulness. Remember, balance is not perfection; it's about finding equilibrium amidst life's fluctuations.

Celebrate the joy of eating without guilt or shame, savoring each bite with gratitude. As you prioritize balance in your diet, you cultivate a harmonious relationship with food and empower yourself to thrive in mind, body, and spirit.

March 7

Overcoming Emotional Eating Triggers

In the journey toward holistic wellness, navigating emotional eating triggers can be a profound challenge. Yet, within each trigger lies an opportunity for growth and empowerment. Pause, breathe, and recognize the emotions stirring within. Seek understanding and compassion for yourself.

Embrace mindful awareness of your triggers, acknowledging their presence without judgment. Then, with steadfast determination, choose to respond with self-care and nourishment that nurtures your body and soul. Remember, you possess the strength and resilience to overcome these triggers, forging a path toward freedom and balance in your relationship with food. Trust in your journey, and embrace the transformative power of self-awareness and self-love.

March 8

Honoring Your Food Choices with Intention

As you navigate your journey towards optimal health, remember the significance of honoring your food choices with intention. Each meal is an opportunity to nourish your body, mind, and spirit. Take a moment to pause and consider the impact of what you consume. Choose foods that align with your health goals and values, and savor each bite mindfully.

By approaching eating with intentionality, you cultivate a deeper connection with your body and cultivate a sense of empowerment over your health. Today, commit to making conscious choices that support your well-being, knowing that each decision brings you closer to vitality and wholeness.

March 9

Mindful Snacking: Savoring Every Bite

In the hustle of our days, even our snacks can become mindless routines. Today, let's pause and savor every bite mindfully. Each morsel is a gift, offering nourishment and vitality to our bodies.

As we practice mindfulness in our snacking, let's remember Proverbs 15:17, "Better a small serving of vegetables with love than a fattened calf with hatred." By savoring each bite with gratitude and intention, we honor our bodies and cultivate a deeper connection with the food we eat. Let's embrace the opportunity to nourish ourselves fully, both physically and spiritually, one mindful bite at a time.

March 10

The Role of Hydration in Well-Being

Let's chat about something super important—hydration! When it comes to mindful snacking, water is your best buddy. It's not just about quenching your thirst; it's about fueling your body and mind. So, next time you're tempted to reach for a snack, why not start with a glass of water?

Hydration plays a huge role in your overall well-being, from boosting your energy levels to supporting digestion. Plus, staying hydrated can even help curb those pesky cravings. So, bottoms up! Remember, a well-hydrated you is a happier, healthier you. Cheers to good health and hydrated snacking!

March 11

Celebrating the Diversity of Flavors

Let's take a moment to celebrate the wonderful tapestry of flavors that life has to offer. From the tangy zest of citrus to the comforting warmth of spices, each flavor brings its own unique charm to the table.

As we savor these diverse tastes, let's also remember to nourish our bodies with wholesome ingredients that fuel us from the inside out. Whether you're enjoying a vibrant salad or a hearty stew, embrace the richness of flavor and the nourishment it provides. Cheers to a life filled with delicious and nutritious eats!

March 12

Building Healthy Eating Habits for Life

As we dive into the journey of building healthy eating habits, let's approach it with a sense of excitement and curiosity. Remember, it's not about strict diets or deprivation, but rather about nourishing our bodies and souls with foods that fuel us. Let's explore new recipes, savoring each bite mindfully.

Celebrate progress, not perfection, and embrace the occasional indulgence guilt-free. Together, let's cultivate a lifestyle where healthy choices come naturally, supporting our overall well-being and vitality. With every meal, we're one step closer to a healthier, happier version of ourselves. Let's savor the journey to lifelong wellness!

March 13

Practicing Portion Control with Awareness

Navigating portion control can be a real challenge, trust me, I've been there too. Snacks have this sneaky way of disappearing faster than we realize. But let's pause for a sec and bring some awareness into the mix.

Next time you reach for a snack, let's take a moment to tune in. Ask yourself, "Am I eating because I'm truly hungry or just out of habit?" Being mindful of our portions can help us enjoy our snacks without overdoing it. So let's savor each bite, knowing that balance and awareness are key to nourishing our bodies and minds.

March 14

Nourishing Your Body, Mind, and Spirit

As you embark on your journey to nourish your body, mind, and spirit, remember that each step you take is a sacred one. Trust in the divine wisdom that guides you toward wellness. Nurture your body with wholesome foods, your mind with positive thoughts, and your spirit with faith-filled intentions.

Embrace the interconnectedness of these elements, recognizing that true health encompasses more than just physical well-being. Let your actions be a reflection of your reverence for the miraculous vessel that is your body, the infinite potential of your mind, and the eternal light within your spirit.

March 15

Mindful Eating in Social Settings

Navigating social gatherings can be challenging when it comes to mindful eating. But guess what? You've got this! Take a moment before diving into that buffet or reaching for seconds to check in with yourself. Ask, "Am I truly hungry or just eating out of habit?"

Remember, it's okay to enjoy the food and company without overindulging. Savor each bite, engage in conversation, and listen to your body's cues. By being present and mindful, you can strike a balance between enjoying yourself and honoring your health goals. So, dig in, connect, and nourish both body and soul.

March 16

Mindful Grocery Shopping and Meal Planning

Picture this: strolling down the aisles, picking vibrant veggies and wholesome grains, each choice a step towards nourishing your body. Meal planning becomes an adventure, not a chore. Embrace the joy of selecting ingredients that fuel your vitality and well-being.

It's not just about what you eat—it's about how you care for yourself. So, next time you're at the store, let mindfulness guide your choices. Remember, every nutritious purchase is an investment in your health journey. Have fun!

March 17

Understanding Food Labels and Ingredients

Ever puzzled over those cryptic food labels? Today, let's unravel the mystery! Take a peek at those ingredient lists—spot any sneaky additives? Learn to navigate the labels like a pro. Your health journey is about making informed choices. Together, let's decode the jargon, empowering you to fuel your body wisely. It's not just about calories, but quality too.

Choose foods that nourish and energize you. Remember, knowledge is power—when you understand what's in your food, you're one step closer to a healthier you. Let's dive in and uncover the secrets hiding in plain sight on those labels!

March 18

Finding Pleasure in Eating Mindfully

Picture this: savoring each bite, feeling grateful for nourishing your body, and relishing the flavors dancing on your taste buds. That's the essence of mindful eating. It's not about restrictions or rules; it's about reconnecting with the joy of eating.

So, take a moment before you dig in. Appreciate the effort that went into preparing your meal. Notice the textures, aromas, and tastes. Let every mouthful be an experience to cherish. When you eat mindfully, you nourish not just your body but also your soul. So, embrace the pleasure of eating and savor every delicious moment.

March 19

Eating with Awareness: Mindful Dining Practices

Dig in, not just to your meal, but into the experience itself. Let every bite be a moment of connection with your body and your food. Pay attention to textures, flavors, and how you feel as you eat. Mindful dining isn't just about what's on your plate; it's about savoring the whole experience.

So slow down, breathe, and enjoy each delicious moment. By eating with awareness, you nourish not just your body, but your soul too. It's a small act of self-care that can have a big impact on your overall well-being. Bon appétit!

March 20

Connecting with Your Food's Origins

Ever stopped to think about where your food comes from? It's more than just what's on your plate—it's a connection to the earth and the people who grow it. Whether it's a crisp apple from a nearby orchard or a vibrant salad straight from the garden, there's something special about knowing the journey of your food.

So, take a moment to appreciate the origins of your meals. It's not just about nourishing your body; it's about honoring the hands that cultivate it and the earth that provides. Let that connection deepen your appreciation for every bite you take.

March 21

Mindful Eating for Energy and Vitality

Feeling sluggish lately? Let's chat about mindful eating! It's not just about what you eat, but how you eat it. When you savor each bite, you're giving your body the fuel it needs to thrive.

Skip the mindless munching and pay attention to your body's hunger cues. Nourish yourself with whole, nutritious foods that energize and invigorate. Trust me, your body will thank you for it! Let's make mindful eating a daily habit for boundless energy and vitality. You can do it!

March 22

Breaking Free from Diet Mentality

So, let's chat about breaking free from that whole diet mentality. It's time to ditch the labels and embrace a healthier relationship with food. Instead of counting calories or restricting yourself, focus on nourishing your body with wholesome, satisfying meals.

Listen to what your body really needs and honor its signals. Remember, it's not about deprivation—it's about abundance and feeling your best. So, let's kick those diet rules to the curb and step into a lifestyle that's all about balance, joy, and loving the skin you're in.

March 23

Mindful Eating for Stress Management

Ever noticed how stress can affect what and how we eat? It's like our emotions take over, leading us to seek comfort in food. But here's the thing: mindful eating can help. When we pause to savor each bite, tuning into our body's signals, we can better manage stress.

So, next time you're feeling overwhelmed, take a deep breath, slow down, and truly enjoy your meal. Let it nourish not just your body, but also your mind and soul. Remember, food is not just fuel; it's a source of comfort and connection. Choose wisely, eat mindfully, and stress less.

March 24

Honoring Your Body's Nutritional Needs

Feeding your body isn't just about filling up; it's about nourishing it with what it needs to thrive. Listen to those hunger cues, choose foods that fuel you, and savor every bite. Whether it's a crisp apple or a hearty salad, honor your body's nutritional needs.

Remember, it's not about restriction; it's about finding balance and giving your body the love it deserves. So, as you reach for your next meal, consider what will truly nourish you from the inside out. Your body will thank you for it, and you'll feel the difference in every aspect of your life.

March 25

Mindful Eating and Digestive Health

As we delve into the realm of mindful eating and digestive health, let's keep it real: our bodies are our temples, and what we fuel them with matters. Take a sec to appreciate the journey of every bite—savor the flavors, feel the nourishment.

Digestive health isn't just about what goes in; it's about how we honor our bodies. So, let's show our guts some love by listening to what they're saying. Let's ditch the guilt trips and embrace balance. Remember, it's not about perfection—it's about progress. Here's to a journey of mindful munching and gut gratitude!

March 26

Overcoming Guilt and Shame around Food Choices

Navigating guilt and shame surrounding food choices can feel overwhelming, but you're not alone in this journey. Remember, it's okay to indulge occasionally; life's about balance, not perfection. Instead of dwelling on past slip-ups, focus on progress and self-compassion.

Treat yourself with kindness, like you would a friend. Every choice is a chance to learn and grow. Embrace healthier habits without punishing yourself for occasional treats. Release the guilt, for it doesn't serve your well-being. You're resilient, capable, and deserving of nourishment that nurtures both body and soul. Keep moving forward with grace and self-love.

March 27

Mindful Eating for Weight Management

Picture this: a journey where every bite is savored, every meal a celebration of nourishment. Mindful eating isn't just about what's on your plate; it's a lifestyle. It's about tuning in to your body's signals, honoring your hunger, and choosing foods that fuel your well-being.

Let's ditch the diet mentality and embrace a more holistic approach to weight management. No more guilt or restrictions—just mindful choices and self-care. Remember, it's not about perfection; it's about progress. So, let's take it one bite at a time, nourishing our bodies, minds, and souls along the way.

March 28

Gratitude for the Abundance of Nutritious Foods

Gratitude fills our hearts as we ponder the wealth of nourishing foods around us. Take a moment to appreciate the vibrant colors, enticing aromas, and wholesome flavors that grace your plate. These gifts from nature not only fuel our bodies but also nourish our souls. Let's savor each bite with mindfulness and appreciation, recognizing the nourishment and vitality they provide.

As we cultivate gratitude for the abundance of nutritious foods, we cultivate a deeper connection to our well-being. Let's embrace this bounty with joy and thanksgiving, knowing that each meal is an opportunity to honor our health and vitality.

March 29

Mindful Eating for Better Sleep and Recovery

Mindful eating isn't just about what you put in your body—it's also about how it affects your overall well-being, including sleep and recovery. When you nourish yourself with intention, choosing foods that promote relaxation and restoration, you set the stage for a better night's sleep and enhanced recovery.

So tonight, savor a soothing cup of herbal tea or a light, nutrient-rich meal. Pay attention to how it makes you feel physically and mentally. As you wind down for the night, let your body rest and rejuvenate, knowing that you've taken a step towards better sleep and recovery.

March

Reflecting on Your Relationship with Food

As you take a moment to think about your connection with food, consider how it makes you feel. Are you nourishing your body with foods that energize and uplift you? Or do you find yourself turning to comfort foods in times of stress? Reflect on the role food plays in your life and how it impacts your overall well-being. Remember, it's not about perfection but progress.

Every choice you make is an opportunity to cultivate a healthier relationship with food. Be kind to yourself, listen to your body's cues, and strive for balance and moderation in your eating habits.

March 31

Celebrating Your Journey to Healthier Eating Habits

Let's end the month with a celebration of your journey to healthier eating habits! Reflect on how far you've come, from making small changes to embracing a lifestyle centered on nourishing your body. Every choice you make matters, and each step forward is a victory. Take a moment to acknowledge your progress, no matter how small, and be proud of yourself.

Remember, this journey is about progress, not perfection. Keep listening to your body, honoring its needs, and making choices that support your well-being. You're doing amazing, and I'm cheering you on every step of the way!

April

—

Embracing Change and Growth

April 1

Embracing the Winds of Change

Amidst April's breeze, let's chat about embracing change. Life's like a gusty wind, unpredictable yet invigorating. It might ruffle our feathers, but it also brings renewal. Think of a tree, swaying with each gust, yet firmly rooted. That's us—flexible, resilient, and ready to grow. Change isn't always easy, but it's where growth happens.

So, instead of resisting, let's welcome it, arms wide open. Embrace the new opportunities, the fresh perspectives, and the chance to bloom in unexpected ways. Let's ride the winds of change, knowing they'll carry us to new and exciting destinations on our journey of life.

April 2

Blossoming Through Transition

In the beautiful chaos of life, April reminds us of the power of transition. Just as flowers bloom from the earth, we too can blossom through change. It's about embracing the unknown, trusting in God's plan, and allowing ourselves to grow.

Yes, transitions can be daunting, but they also bring new beginnings, fresh opportunities, and profound growth. So, let's lean into this season of change with faith and courage. Remember, God is with us every step of the way, nurturing our roots, and guiding us towards the light. Embrace the journey, dear ones, and watch how you flourish.

April 3

Rooted in Resilience

In this month, we're all about growth. Life throws curveballs, but we're resilient. Like a sturdy tree, our roots run deep. Challenges come and go, but we stand strong. It's about facing adversity with courage, knowing that storms make us stronger.

We bend, but we don't break. Every setback is just a setup for a comeback. So, let's embrace change, knowing that it's part of our journey. Through it all, we're rooted in resilience. Let's keep pushing forward, growing, and blooming. Remember, we're capable of weathering any storm that comes our way. Together, we rise.

April 4

Nurturing New Beginnings

In the grand tapestry of life, this month whispers of fresh starts and budding possibilities. Just as the earth awakens from its slumber, so too can we embrace new beginnings with faith and hope.

It's a time to nurture the seeds of change planted within us, trusting that they will bloom in due season. Let us release the weight of past seasons and step boldly into the unknown, knowing that God is our constant companion on this journey of growth. May we find solace in His promise of renewal, and may our hearts be open to the abundant blessings He has in store.

April 5

Thriving Amidst Transformation

Haven't we all found ourselves in seasons of change? April whispers tales of transformation, inviting us to thrive amidst the shifting winds. Like flowers blooming from the rain-kissed earth, we too can embrace growth amid uncertainty.

It's in these moments of transformation that our true strength emerges. Let's dance with the rhythm of change, knowing that within each shift lies opportunity. As we navigate the twists and turns of life's journey, may we find solace in the knowledge that we are resilient beings, capable of blossoming even in the most unexpected of circumstances. Embrace the change, and watch yourself thrive.

April 6

Welcoming Change with Open Arms

Today, let's welcome the fresh breeze of opportunity with arms wide open! Just like the blossoming flowers eagerly greet the warmth of spring, let's embrace the chance to grow and flourish in our own lives.

Maybe it's trying something new, like a hobby or a skill, or perhaps it's letting go of old habits to make room for positive ones. Whatever it is, let's approach it with excitement and curiosity. Remember, every step we take towards growth brings us closer to the vibrant life we're meant to live. So let's step forward with open hearts and open minds!

April 7

Finding Strength in Adaptation

Amidst April's ever-changing scenery, let's explore the art of adaptation. Life's like a blooming garden, full of surprises and growth spurts. When faced with unexpected twists, we're not just surviving – we're thriving. It's about bending without breaking, embracing the rhythm of change. Like a resilient tree swaying in the breeze, we find our strength in flexibility.

Each challenge, a chance to evolve, to blossom into something more vibrant than before. So, let's dance in April's rain, knowing we're growing stronger with every step. Here's to adapting, flourishing, and embracing the beauty of transformation.

April 8

Sowing Seeds of Possibility

In the garden of life, this month brings forth the promise of new beginnings. Just as a gardener sows seeds in the fertile soil, we too have the opportunity to sow seeds of possibility in our lives. As we plant our dreams and aspirations, let us trust in the divine timing of growth.

Even when the ground seems barren, have faith that beneath the surface, seeds are germinating, preparing to burst forth into vibrant life. May we nurture our seeds with patience and perseverance, knowing that in due time, they will bloom into beautiful manifestations of God's grace and abundance.

April 9

Rising to New Heights

As we journey through life, we're often met with seasons of change. Just like the blossoming flowers of spring, we too have the opportunity to grow and flourish. Embracing change can be daunting, but it's also where we find new opportunities for growth.

Remember, God's plans for us are greater than we could ever imagine. So, let's rise to new heights with faith and courage. Let's trust that even in the midst of uncertainty, God is leading us towards something beautiful. May we embrace each step of this journey, knowing that with Him, we can soar to unimaginable heights.

April 10

Transforming Challenges into Opportunities

Let me remind you that you're absolutely killing it! I know this month we have been focusing on transforming challenges into opportunities, and let me tell you, you're doing an amazing job at it.

Every hurdle you face? It's just another chance for you to shine brighter and grow stronger. So keep pushing forward, keep that positive attitude going, and remember, you've got what it takes to turn any setback into a setup for success. You're unstoppable, and I couldn't be prouder of you.

April 11

Embracing the Journey of Growth

On this twelfth day of April, let's infuse our journey of growth with a sense of joy and excitement. Embrace the idea that growth can be a thrilling adventure, full of unexpected twists and turns. Just as a seedling eagerly stretches towards the sun, let us eagerly reach towards our own potential.

Cultivate a mindset that sees challenges as opportunities for growth and views setbacks as stepping stones to success. Remember, the process of growth is not always easy, but it is always worth it. So, let's embark on this journey with enthusiasm and a spirit of curiosity, ready to embrace all that lies ahead.

April 12

Cultivating Inner Renewal

On this day, let's infuse our journey of growth with a sense of joy and adventure. Cultivating inner renewal isn't just about serious introspection—it's about embracing the process with a light heart and a spirit of playfulness. Imagine each step forward as a dance, each challenge as an opportunity to learn something new.

Let's explore the depths of our being with curiosity and enthusiasm, knowing that every moment holds the potential for transformation. Embrace the beauty of renewal, and let the journey unfold with a sense of wonder and excitement. Growth can be fun—let's make it so!

April 13

Turning Over a New Leaf

On this day, embrace the opportunity to turn over a new leaf. Let go of old habits, doubts, and fears that no longer serve you. Embrace change with courage and determination, knowing that every step forward brings growth and transformation.

Like a tree shedding its old leaves to make room for new growth, allow yourself to release what holds you back and step into a brighter, more empowered future. Embrace the beauty of renewal and the promise of new beginnings. Today marks the start of a chapter filled with possibility, resilience, and the unwavering belief in your own potential.

April 14

Stepping into Your Power

Today, may you find strength in your faith as you step into the power that resides within you. Remember that you are a vessel of divine purpose, filled with limitless potential and grace. Allow the light of God's love to guide your path and empower you to overcome any obstacles that stand in your way.

Embrace your calling with courage and conviction, knowing that you are supported by the hands of the Almighty. Step boldly into your destiny, for you are equipped with everything you need to fulfill God's plan for your life.

April 15

Embracing the Unknown

Let's embrace the unknown today with open hearts and courageous spirits. It's natural to feel fear when stepping into uncharted territory, but remember, growth often lies just beyond our comfort zones. Today, let's take a leap of faith and pursue that dream we've been nurturing in our hearts.

Trust in your abilities, believe in the journey ahead, and know that you are capable of achieving greatness. As we embrace the unknown, let's find strength in our resilience and excitement in the endless possibilities that await us on the other side. Let's step boldly into the future, knowing that every step forward brings us closer to our dreams.

April 16

Discovering Hidden Potential

Today, let's embrace the journey of discovery. Don't let fear hold you back; instead, take a leap of faith towards uncovering your hidden potential. It's time to step out of your comfort zone and explore the vast possibilities that await. Trust in yourself and your abilities.

With courage as your compass, venture into the unknown and unlock new realms of growth and fulfillment. You possess untapped talents and strengths waiting to be unleashed. Embrace this moment as an opportunity to shine brightly and soar to new heights. Your potential is boundless—embrace it wholeheartedly.

April 17

Growing Through Adversity

Start or end the day with reflection, on the transformative power of faith amidst adversity. In times of challenge, remember Romans 8:28, "And we know that in all things God works for the good of those who love him, who have been called according to his purpose." Even in the toughest seasons, God is at work, shaping and molding us into who we're meant to be.

Embrace the trials, for they are opportunities for growth and refinement. Through faith, we not only endure adversity but emerge stronger and more resilient than ever before. Trust in God's plan and keep growing, for He is with you always.

April 18

Harnessing the Power of Change

As we reflect on our journey of growth, ask yourself: do you have a healthy relationship with change? Change is the essence of life, a constant force shaping our path. Embrace it with open arms, for it brings opportunities for renewal and transformation.

In the face of uncertainty, find strength in your resilience and adaptability. Trust in the process, knowing that every twist and turn leads to growth. Embrace change as a catalyst for personal evolution, and watch as it propels you towards new heights of fulfillment and purpose. Embrace change, and let it guide you towards your brightest future.

April 19

Fostering Personal Evolution Affirmation

I am committed to fostering my personal evolution. Each day, I embrace growth, learning, and transformation. I welcome change as an opportunity for self-discovery and improvement. With an open heart and a resilient spirit, I navigate life's challenges with grace and courage.

I trust in my ability to adapt and thrive in any circumstance. I honor my journey, celebrating both my triumphs and setbacks as valuable lessons along the way. With each step forward, I become more aligned with my true self, empowered to create the life I desire. I am evolving, expanding, and embracing my fullest potential.

April 20

Journeying Through the Ebb and Flow

In life, we journey through seasons of ebb and flow—moments of abundance and moments of scarcity, times of joy and times of sorrow. Yet, within this rhythm lies a profound truth: each phase is integral to our growth. Just as the tide recedes to reveal hidden treasures, so do our challenges unveil our inner strength and resilience.

Embrace the ebb and flow of life with faith and courage, knowing that every high tide brings blessings, and every low tide brings lessons. Trust in the divine timing of your journey, for amidst the shifting currents, you are guided towards greater purpose and fulfillment.

April 21

Discovering Splendor in Metamorphosis

Let's chat about the beauty of transformation. Life's like a caterpillar turning into a butterfly - messy but magnificent. Embrace change; it's where growth thrives. Each hurdle, each shift, leads to something beautiful. So, when things feel topsy-turvy, remember you're in the midst of your own metamorphosis.

Your struggles are shaping you into something extraordinary. It's like a caterpillar shedding its cocoon, revealing vibrant wings ready to soar. Embrace this process, for within it lies your true splendor. So, spread those wings and fly, dear friend. Your journey is just beginning, and it's nothing short of breathtaking.

April 22

Progress Through Introspection

Let's take a moment to dive inward. Progress doesn't always mean moving forward physically; sometimes, it's about looking within. Introspection is key—it's like polishing a mirror to see our true selves. When we pause to reflect, we grow. Ask yourself: What am I learning? How am I evolving?

Trust that God is guiding this journey. Embrace the insights gained, the lessons learned. Remember, the path to spiritual growth often starts with a single, honest look inside. So, let's journey within today, and may we emerge stronger, wiser, and more aligned with our faith.

April 23

Unveiling Your True Self

Today's about getting real. You know, stripping away the layers, the masks, all that stuff. It's time to embrace the raw, unfiltered you. Let go of the need to impress or conform. Be authentically, unapologetically yourself.

It's in that vulnerability that you'll find your true strength and beauty. So, let's drop the act, shall we? Embrace your quirks, your flaws, your uniqueness. Because guess what? That's what makes you, well, you. And trust me, the world needs more of that.

April 24

Adopting a Mindset of Progress

We need to talk about adopting a mindset of progress. Life's all about moving forward, even if it's just a small step each day. Embrace change, learn from it, and keep pushing yourself to grow.

Celebrate your victories, no matter how small, and remember that every effort counts. It's not about perfection; it's about progress. So, take a deep breath, trust the process, and keep moving forward. You've got this!

April 25

Wholeheartedly Embracing Life's Shifts

As we journey through life, we're bound to encounter shifts and changes. It's easy to resist, but what if we embraced them wholeheartedly? Just like trees swaying in the wind, we can learn to bend without breaking.

Trusting in God's plan, we can navigate transitions with courage and faith. Instead of fearing the unknown, let's welcome it as an opportunity for growth. So, as life's shifts come your way, remember that God is with you every step of the journey. Embrace them wholeheartedly, knowing that they're leading you closer to where you're meant to be.

April 26

Inviting Fresh Horizons

How about today you embrace the idea of inviting fresh horizons. It's about stepping into new opportunities with faith and courage. Just like a sunrise brings a new day, let's welcome the dawn of fresh beginnings. Trust that God is leading us to greater heights, even if the path seems uncertain.

Let's release the fear of the unknown and walk boldly into the future, knowing that with each step, we're drawing closer to the amazing plans He has in store for us. So let's lift our heads high and embrace the adventure ahead!

April 27

Adopting a Mindset of Expansion

So, today's all about opening up to new possibilities, you know? It's like stretching your wings and embracing the unknown. Instead of holding back, why not lean into growth? Trust me, the world's full of surprises waiting for you to explore.

So, let's ditch those limits and dive headfirst into the adventure of life. It's all about seeing things from a fresh perspective, breaking free from the old, and stepping into something bigger and better. You've got this!

April 28

Reflection: Fertile Ground for Growth

As we kick back on this day, let's talk about reflection. It's like digging deep into the soil of your life, uncovering the roots and shoots of who you are. Take a sec to ponder where you've been, where you're at, and where you're headed.

It's all about recognizing the lessons learned, the victories won, and the challenges overcome. Every bit of dirt you sift through is fertile ground for growth. So, let's dig in, embrace the messiness, and nurture those seeds of wisdom.

April 29

Blooming into Your True Self

As April wraps up, let's reflect on how far we've come. Just like flowers blooming into their true selves, we too are on a journey of growth and transformation. It's about embracing change, facing challenges, and blossoming into the beautiful souls we were meant to be.

Remember, God's hand is guiding us every step of the way. So, as we bid farewell to April, let's carry this newfound wisdom into the days ahead. Keep blooming, keep shining, and keep trusting in the plan He has for you. The best is yet to come!

April 30

Embracing the End of April

With just one day left in April, let's make it count. Take some time to slow down and appreciate the simple joys that surround you. Whether it's the warmth of the sun on your face or the laughter of loved ones, cherish each moment as if it were a precious gift.

Reflect on the lessons you've learned this month and how they've helped you grow. And as you bid farewell to April, look forward to the adventures that await in the month ahead. Remember, every ending is a new beginning, so let's welcome May with open arms and hopeful hearts.

May

Cultivating Gratitude and Positivity

May 1

Grateful Heart, Positive Mind

In the journey of life, a grateful heart becomes the beacon that guides us through both light and shadow. With every breath, we find reasons to offer thanks, fostering a positive mindset that illuminates our path. Gratitude transforms ordinary moments into extraordinary blessings, infusing each day with hope, joy, and abundance.

As we cultivate a grateful heart, we discover the power to shift our perspective, embracing challenges as opportunities for growth and setbacks as stepping stones toward greater resilience. With a heart overflowing with gratitude and a mind filled with positivity, we navigate life's twists and turns with grace, courage, and unwavering faith.

May 2

Planting Seeds of Thankfulness

Happy May 2nd! Today's all about planting seeds of thankfulness. Take a sec to appreciate the little things—like that first sip of coffee or a sunny sky. Let's spread gratitude vibes everywhere we go, watering those seeds with love.

Remember, it's those small moments that bloom into big blessings. So, whether you're tackling a mountain of work or just chilling, find something to be thankful for. Let's make today awesome together!

May 3

Radiate Positivity, Embrace Blessings

On this beautiful day, let's take a moment to soak in all the goodness around us. Radiate positivity like sunshine, spreading warmth and joy wherever you go. Embrace the blessings that come your way, big or small. Remember, even during challenges, there's always something to be grateful for. Let your faith be your guiding light, filling your heart with hope and courage.

Trust that brighter days are ahead and keep shining your light for others to see. You're stronger than you know, and with faith, you can overcome anything. Blessings abound, my friend.

May 4

Gratitude: The Key to Joyful Living

Listen, beautiful soul let's chat about something that can totally transform your life: gratitude. Seriously, it's like the secret sauce to living a joyful life. When we take a sec to count our blessings and appreciate the little things, it's like everything just falls into place.

So, let's take a moment today to reflect on all the goodness in our lives. Whether it's a warm cup of coffee, a kind word from a friend, or a beautiful sunrise, there's always something to be thankful for. Let's spread that gratitude vibe everywhere we go!

May 5

Finding Beauty in Every Moment

You know what's awesome? Finding beauty in every moment. Seriously, take a sec and think about it. From that first sip of coffee in the morning to the sunset at night, there's so much to be thankful for. It's like life's little reminders that there's good stuff all around us, you know?

So, next time you're feeling a bit down, just pause, look around, and find something to be grateful for. Trust me, it'll totally shift your perspective and bring a smile to your face. Embrace that gratitude, my friend—it's like sunshine for the soul.

May 6

Nurturing a Spirit of Appreciation

Today remember that gratitude isn't just a word; it's a way of life. It's about appreciating the little things—the sun on your face, the laughter of loved ones, the scent of freshly brewed coffee. It's taking a moment to say "thank you" for all the blessings, big and small, that fill your days.

So, nurture that spirit of appreciation within you. Pause, take a deep breath, and soak in the goodness that surrounds you. Because when we live with gratitude, every day feels brighter, every challenge feels conquerable, and every moment feels like a gift.

May 7

Positivity: Your Inner Light

Gratitude and positivity, they're like the sunshine for your soul. When you're feeling thankful, when you're radiating positivity, that's when your inner light shines the brightest. It's like you're tapping into this divine energy, this beautiful connection with something greater than yourself.

So, embrace gratitude, soak up the positivity, and let your inner light illuminate the world around you. You never know whose day you might brighten, whose heart you might touch just by being authentically you. Keep shining, keep spreading love, and remember, your light matters more than you know.

May 8

The Ripple Effect of Gratitude

"This Ripple Effect of Gratitude" reminds us of the profound impact gratitude has not only on our own lives but also on those around us. When we cultivate a heart of thankfulness, our attitude shifts, and positivity radiates outward, touching the lives of others.

Each act of gratitude creates a ripple, spreading joy, kindness, and hope to those we encounter. As we embrace the practice of gratitude, we become catalysts for positive change, influencing the world around us one thankful thought at a time. Let us be mindful of the ripple effect of our gratitude and the power it holds to transform lives.

May 9

Overflowing with Appreciation

Let's go on a journey of embracing life's abundance with a heart brimming with gratitude. As you navigate the pages of this devotional, you'll discover the power of appreciating the small blessings that surround you each day. From the warmth of the morning sun to the laughter of loved ones, every moment becomes an opportunity to express gratitude.

Through reflection, prayer, and inspirational messages, you'll cultivate a spirit of thankfulness that overflows into every aspect of your life. Join in this transformative journey and experience the joy of living in a state of perpetual appreciation.

May 10

Blessings in Disguise: Finding Gratitude in Unexpected Places

Today, let embark on a journey of discovery, recognizing the hidden blessings that await in the most unexpected places. Life's twists and turns often conceal valuable lessons, growth opportunities, and moments of profound grace.

As you cultivate a spirit of gratitude, begin to unveil the blessings in disguise—those moments that challenge you, shape you, and ultimately lead you closer to your purpose. With open hearts and minds, embrace the journey, trusting that even in the midst of adversity, blessings abound. May you find gratitude in every circumstance and joy in the unfolding of life's divine plan.

May 11

Morning Reflections: Starting Your Day with Gratitude

Today, as you awaken to the dawn of a new day, pause for a moment of reflection. Amidst life's hustle and bustle, may you find solace in the simple act of gratitude. Look around you, notice the beauty of the world awakening, and embrace the gift of another day.

Even in the midst of challenges, there are blessings waiting to be discovered. Let gratitude be your guiding light, illuminating the path ahead with hope and joy. As you start your day with a heart full of thankfulness, may you attract abundance, positivity, and blessings in disguise.

May 12

Faith-Filled Thankfulness: Trusting in Divine Provision

Today, my friend, as you awaken to a new dawn, let your heart overflow with gratitude. In every moment, amidst life's twists and turns, there are hidden blessings waiting to be uncovered. Embrace each challenge as an opportunity for growth, each setback as a stepping stone to something greater.

Trust in the divine provision that surrounds you, knowing that every trial you face is shaping you into the person you are meant to be. Open your eyes to the beauty of the journey, for even in the darkest of times, there is light. May your day be filled with faith-filled thankfulness.

May 13

Counting Blessings: Gratitude as a Daily Practice

Today, dear friend, I urge you to embark on a journey of gratitude. As you navigate the twists and turns of life, take a moment to pause and reflect on the blessings surrounding you. Even in the midst of challenges, there are countless reasons to be thankful.

Embrace each day as an opportunity to cultivate gratitude as a daily practice. By counting your blessings, you'll uncover the beauty hidden in everyday moments. Let gratitude become your guiding light, illuminating your path with joy and contentment. Embrace each blessing, big or small, and watch as your heart overflows with appreciation for the abundant gifts of life.

May1 4

Grace Upon Grace: Embracing God's Abundant Love

Today, as you awaken to a new day, may you be reminded of the abundant grace that surrounds you. In every moment, God's love flows freely, offering comfort, strength, and hope. Embrace the challenges that come your way, knowing that they are opportunities for growth and transformation.

Trust in the divine plan that unfolds before you, for every trial is a stepping stone toward a brighter tomorrow. As you navigate life's journey, may you be filled with gratitude for the blessings in disguise, and may you experience the boundless love and grace of our Creator in every step you take.

May 15

Joyful Surrender: Letting Go and Letting God

Today, embrace the liberating power of surrender. Release the burdens weighing heavy on your heart and entrust them to the loving hands of God. As you relinquish control, you open yourself to a profound sense of peace and joy. Surrender is not a sign of weakness but a courageous act of faith. Let go of the need to orchestrate every detail of your life and instead, surrender to the divine plan unfolding before you.

In surrender, you will find freedom, serenity, and a deeper connection to the source of all joy. Trust in God's guidance and embrace the journey with joyful surrender.

May 16

A Heart of Gratitude: Cultivating Thankfulness in Every Season

Today, awaken to the beauty of gratitude. In every season of life, there are blessings waiting to be discovered. Pause and reflect on the abundance that surrounds you. Even amidst challenges, there is much to be thankful for. Cultivate a heart of gratitude, allowing it to permeate every aspect of your being. As you embrace thankfulness, you'll find joy in the simplest of moments and strength in the toughest of times.

Let gratitude be your guiding light, illuminating your path with positivity and grace. With a heart full of gratitude, you'll discover the true richness of life in every season.

May 17

The Power of Positive Thinking: Transforming Perspectives

Today, recognize the transformative power of positive thinking. Shift your perspective from doubt to belief, from fear to courage. Choose to see the beauty in every situation, even amidst challenges. Your thoughts shape your reality, so fill your mind with positivity and optimism. Embrace the power of gratitude and focus on the blessings in your life.

As you cultivate a positive mindset, you'll attract abundance, joy, and fulfillment. Trust in the journey ahead, knowing that your thoughts have the power to create the life you desire. With a mindset rooted in positivity, you can overcome any obstacle and embrace the beauty of life.

May 18

Living in Gratitude: Finding Contentment in Every Circumstance

Conflict can be a friend or an enemy but choose to confront conflict with a heart full of gratitude. In moments of tension and discord, choose to see the blessings hidden within. Shift your focus from grievances to gratitude, finding contentment amidst every circumstance.

Embrace empathy and understanding, seeking common ground with those you disagree with. Let gratitude be your guiding light, illuminating the path towards reconciliation and peace. As you cultivate a spirit of thankfulness, you'll discover the power to transform conflict into opportunities for growth and connection. With gratitude as your anchor, navigate the complexities of relationships with grace and humility, finding contentment in every interaction.

May 19

Faith-Fueled Optimism: Seeing the Good in All Things

Let me share a real-life example of faith-fueled optimism. Despite facing setbacks and challenges, a close friend of mine maintained an unwavering belief in the goodness of life. When she lost her job unexpectedly, instead of succumbing to despair, she viewed it as an opportunity for growth.

With faith as her guide, she remained optimistic, trusting that something better awaited her. Through perseverance and positivity, she landed a new job that not only provided financial stability but also brought her immense joy. Her story reminds us that faith-fueled optimism can turn obstacles into stepping stones towards a brighter future.

May 20

Sacred Moments: Finding God in the Ordinary

Today, cherish the sacred moments of one-on-one time with yourself or a loved one. In the hustle and bustle of life, carve out precious moments for connection and reflection. Whether it's a quiet walk in nature or a heartfelt conversation over coffee, embrace the beauty of being present in the moment.

These ordinary moments hold the potential for divine encounters, where God's presence is felt in the simplicity of human connection. As you cherish these sacred moments, you'll discover a deeper sense of gratitude and fulfillment, recognizing the holiness woven into the fabric of everyday life.

May 21

Grateful Hearts, Generous Spirits: Sharing Love and Kindness

Today, take a moment to pause and reflect on the beauty of life itself. Amidst the hustle and bustle, let gratitude fill your heart for the gift of each new day. As you journey through life, embrace the power of a grateful heart and a generous spirit.

Share love and kindness with those around you, extending compassion and understanding to all. In the simple acts of kindness, you'll find fulfillment and purpose, enriching not only your own life but the lives of others as well. Let gratitude guide your steps and generosity be your legacy as you navigate the journey of life.

May 22

Trusting the Journey: Finding Peace in Uncertain Times

As you navigate the twists and turns of life's journey, remember that it's okay to feel uncertain. Trusting the journey can be challenging, especially when faced with adversity and doubt. But even in the midst of uncertainty, hold onto hope and keep moving forward.

Embrace the unknown with courage and faith, knowing that every step you take brings you closer to your destination. Trust in the divine plan that guides your path and find solace in the knowledge that you are never alone. Despite the challenges, may you find peace in the journey and strength in the journey itself.

May 23

Gratitude in Action: Serving Others with Joy

Today, let your heart overflow with gratitude as you embark on a journey of serving others with joy. In every act of kindness, you have the opportunity to make a meaningful difference in someone's life. Whether it's lending a helping hand, offering a listening ear, or sharing a smile, your actions have the power to spread love and compassion.

Embrace the privilege of serving others, knowing that in giving, you receive abundance in return. Let gratitude guide your actions and infuse each moment with purpose and meaning. Together, let us illuminate the world with acts of love and kindness.

May 24

Prayers of Thanksgiving: Expressing Gratitude to God

Today, let your prayers be songs of thanksgiving, lifting your voice to God in gratitude for His countless blessings. With each breath, acknowledge His goodness and faithfulness in your life.

Reflect on the moments of joy, the lessons learned, and the challenges overcome. Offer your heartfelt thanks for His provision and guidance, trusting that He hears every word spoken from your heart. As you express your gratitude, you draw closer to the divine, deepening your relationship with the One who loves you unconditionally. May your prayers of thanksgiving be a source of comfort, strength, and joy as you journey through life.

May 25

Radiant Gratitude: Letting Your Light Shine Bright

Amidst life's challenges, find strength in practicing gratitude. Even in moments of darkness, when it feels impossible to see the light, choose to let your gratitude shine like a beacon of hope. Perhaps you've faced loss, disappointment, or heartache, and gratitude feels out of reach. Yet, in these moments, there is still beauty to be found.

Embrace gratitude as an act of defiance against despair, illuminating the path forward with your radiant light. By acknowledging even the smallest blessings, you affirm your resilience and invite joy into your life. Let your gratitude be a testament to your unwavering spirit and inner strength.

May 26

Overflowing with Appreciation: Celebrating Life's Blessings

Today, take a moment to revel in the abundance of blessings surrounding you. Amidst life's trials and tribulations, pause and recognize the countless reasons to be grateful.

Even in the midst of chaos, there are moments of beauty, love, and grace waiting to be acknowledged. Let your heart overflow with appreciation for the gift of life itself, for the love of family and friends, for the simple joys that bring warmth to your soul.

Celebrate each blessing with gratitude, knowing that by embracing the richness of life, you invite more blessings to unfold. May your spirit be forever filled with appreciation and awe.

May 27

Grateful Hearts, Open Hands: Receiving God's Gifts with Humility

I want to share a personal journey of gratitude after enduring profound loss. Despite the pain and heartache, I've discovered immense blessings amidst the darkness. Through the loss of loved ones, I've learned to cherish every moment and hold onto memories with gratitude.

Even in the depths of grief, I've found solace in the love and support of family and friends, reminding me of the precious gift of companionship. As I navigate life's uncertainties, I strive to keep my heart open and my hands ready to receive God's gifts with humility and gratitude. In every trial, there is a lesson, and in every loss, there is an opportunity to grow in gratitude.

May 28

Divine Encounters: Recognizing God's Presence in Everyday Moments

This is something that I am often reminded of and wanted to share with you about recognizing God's presence in everyday moments. I have my days when I am feeling overwhelmed by the day's challenges, and it can be just a gentle breeze that will brush by me. In that simple gesture of nature, I feel a profound sense of peace that always washes over me.

It's as if God Himself is whispering, "I am here." In those moments, I realize that divine encounters are not reserved for grand occasions but are woven into the fabric of our daily lives. May we open our hearts and minds to recognize these sacred moments and find peace in God's constant presence.

May 29

The Gift of Gratitude: Embracing God's Grace with Thankfulness

Today, let's reflect on the gift of gratitude and the importance of embracing God's grace with thankfulness. In the hustle and bustle of life, it's easy to overlook the blessings that surround us. Yet, when we pause to count our blessings, we find that they are abundant and overflowing.

From the air we breathe to the love of family and friends, each day is filled with reasons to be thankful. Let's cultivate a heart of gratitude, recognizing that every good and perfect gift comes from above. May we embrace God's grace with thankfulness, knowing that He is the source of all our blessings.

May 30

Hearts Full of Praise: Worshiping God with Gratitude

Let's journey together in cultivating hearts full of praise, worshiping God with gratitude. Amidst life's trials and triumphs, let us never forget the countless reasons we have to praise Him. From the beauty of creation to the love that surrounds us, each day offers opportunities to lift our voices in thanksgiving.

Let's not overlook the small blessings in pursuit of the grandiose. Instead, let's find joy in the simple moments and offer them up as offerings of gratitude to our Creator. May our hearts overflow with praise, a testament to His goodness and faithfulness in our lives.

May 31

Embracing New Beginnings

As we reach the end of this month, let us embrace the promise of new beginnings with hearts filled with gratitude and faith. Just as the dawn breaks after the darkest of nights, God offers us the gift of fresh starts and renewed hope.

Let us release the burdens of the past and step forward with courage and trust in His divine plan. May we welcome the opportunities and blessings that await us on this journey, knowing that He who holds the stars in place is guiding our steps. With faith as our compass, let us embrace each new beginning with joy and anticipation.

June

—

Finding Balance and Harmony

June 1

Blooming in Summer's Glow

Can you feel the warmth of the sun on your skin? It's like nature's way of saying, "Hey, it's time to shine!" Just like those flowers out there, we're blooming in the glow of summer.

Embrace the energy, the growth, and the beauty of this season. Let's soak up every moment, every smile, and every bit of joy that comes our way. May this summer be a time of renewal, growth, and abundance in your life. You're blooming, my friend, and it's a beautiful sight to see.

June 2

Sunlit Paths of Growth

In the quiet of morning, as sunlight filters through curtains, pause. Let its warmth envelop you, a gentle reminder of life's beauty. Amidst uncertainty, trust in the journey, for even the smallest steps lead to growth. Embrace these sunlit paths, where shadows fade, replaced by hope.

Each day offers opportunity to bloom, to discover strength within. Allow yourself grace, knowing growth takes time. In moments of doubt, remember the sun's unwavering presence. As you navigate life's twists and turns, may you find solace in its rays, guiding you forward with quiet assurance.

June 3

Nature's Flourishing Beauty

Pause to today to embrace nature's symphony. Let the whisper of the wind and the dance of sunlight on leaves soothe your weary soul. In the delicate petals of a flower, find resilience; in the vast expanse of the sky, find freedom. Allow nature's flourishing beauty to awaken gratitude within, reminding you of the divine in every moment.

With each breath, connect with the earth beneath your feet and the heavens above, feeling the unity of all creation. Today, immerse yourself in the sacred tapestry of life, finding solace, inspiration, and renewal in nature's timeless embrace.

June 4

Celebrating Life's Abundance

In the symphony of existence, hear the melodious chords of divine providence. Each dawn brings forth a new movement, each dusk a serene cadence of gratitude. Amidst life's rhythms, savor the sweet nectar of blessings showered upon you by the Almighty.

With each step, revel in the abundance of grace, the richness of love, and the boundless blessings that adorn your path. Today, let your soul dance to the tune of gratitude as you celebrate the overflowing goodness of life, embracing the divine abundance that surrounds you in every moment, filling your heart with joy and your spirit with peace.

June 5

Warmth and Renewal Within

Here is a little nugget of wisdom for you today. Life can throw some pretty tough stuff our way, right? I get it, trust me. There are moments when it feels like the darkness might never lift, like you're stuck in this endless loop of gloom.

But here's the thing: within you lies a warmth, a light waiting to be reignited. It's that spark of hope, that flicker of resilience that refuses to be snuffed out. So take a deep breath, my friend. Embrace that renewal within you, and remember, you've got this. You're stronger than you know.

June 6

Embracing Outdoor Adventures

You know what's seriously underrated? Getting out there and soaking up some nature. Seriously, it's like hitting the reset button for your soul. Picture this: you, surrounded by the great outdoors, the sun kissing your skin, and the wind whispering through the trees.

It's pure wonderfulness, I tell ya (said in my Regine, from the sitcom "Living Single" voice). Whether it's a hike in the mountains, a stroll on the beach, or even just chilling in your backyard, there's something about being outside that just fills you up, you know? So next time you're feeling a little frazzled, why not lace up those shoes and go on a little adventure? Trust me, your spirit will thank you.

June 7

Joyful Family Gatherings Await

Now this should make your day – those good ol' family BBQs! There's just something magical about firing up the grill, isn't there? The sizzle of the burgers, the tantalizing aroma of the ribs... But it's not just about the food; it's about the memories we make. Picture this: laughter filling the air, kids running around playing games, and adults catching up on life.

It's those moments of togetherness, those heart-to-heart conversations shared over a plate of deliciousness, that make these gatherings truly special. So go ahead, plan that BBQ, gather your loved ones, and let the joy unfold!

June 8

Basking in Sunlight's Radiance

Alright, listen up! It's that time of year again – summer's here, baby! And you know what that means? Beach days, vacations, and all-around sunshine good times! There's nothing quite like feeling the sand between your toes, the warmth of the sun on your skin, and the sound of waves crashing in the background.

So, grab your shades, pack a cooler, and let's head out for some fun in the sun! Whether it's building sandcastles, swimming in the cool waters, or simply lounging on a beach towel with a good book, let's make the most of these sunny days ahead! What are you waiting for, let's go!

June 9

June's Vibrant Energy Unleashed

Please don't tell me you haven't done anything this summer. Get outside and enjoy the day. It's time to embrace the vibrant energy that this month brings, stepping into the sunshine with a spring in our step. Whether it's dancing under the stars, exploring new trails, or simply soaking up the beauty of nature, let's seize every moment with enthusiasm and joy.

Let's make memories that will last a lifetime, laugh until our sides ache, and cherish the simple pleasures that life has to offer. So here's to June – a month filled with endless possibilities and boundless adventures

June 10

Restoring Hope in Darkness

Amidst life's shadows, know you're not alone. It's okay to stumble; we all do. But remember, even in the darkest nights, stars shine brightest. Embrace those moments of despair; they're just pit stops, not permanent residences. Your story isn't over yet; there's still much to unfold. Look within; your resilience is your superpower.

Feel the warmth of hope kindling within you, ready to ignite. You're stronger than you realize, more resilient than you know. So, take a deep breath, gather your courage, and step forward. Remember, even in the darkest tunnels, there's always a glimmer of light.

June 11

Courageous Vulnerability

In life, there's a strength in showing your true self, flaws and all. It's about being brave enough to let others see the real you, even when it's scary. Vulnerability isn't weakness; it's a testament to your courage. It's saying, "Here I am, unapologetically me." So today, let's embrace our vulnerabilities, our quirks, our insecurities.

Let's share our stories, our fears, our hopes. By opening up, we create connections, we inspire others, and we find a deeper sense of belonging. So take a deep breath, summon your courage, and let your light shine through your beautiful vulnerabilities.

June 12

Celebrating Small Victories

Today's the day to give yourself a high-five for those little wins! Whether it's getting out of bed on time or finally finishing that daunting task, every victory counts. Take a moment to acknowledge your progress and the effort you've put in.

It's these small victories that pave the way for bigger successes. So, celebrate with a smile, a fist pump, or a little dance—whatever feels right for you. Remember, life's journey is made up of these moments, so savor them and keep moving forward with confidence. You're doing amazing things, one small victory at a time!

June 13

Embracing Change Gracefully

Amidst life's twists and turns, remember to ride the waves with a sense of grace. Change can be daunting, but it also offers us a chance to grow and evolve. Embrace the unknown with open arms, knowing that every challenge carries within it the seeds of opportunity.

Trust in your ability to adapt and thrive, even in the face of uncertainty. Allow yourself the freedom to let go of what no longer serves you and welcome in the new with courage and resilience. Change is the heartbeat of life; let's dance to its rhythm with grace and gratitude.

June 14

Living with Purpose

In life's tapestry, find your thread and weave it boldly. Today, embrace the journey with open arms and a heart full of passion. Each step, each choice, contributes to the masterpiece you're crafting. So, laugh with abandon, dream without limits, and dance to the rhythm of your own song. Let your purpose be the compass guiding your adventures.

When doubt whispers, drown it out with determination. Remember, you're the author of your story, so write it with intention and live it with unwavering courage. Embrace the beauty of the unknown, for within it lies the magic of possibility.

June 15

Savoring Life's Simple Pleasures

Take a moment today, breathe in deeply, and pause. Notice the sunlight filtering through the leaves, the gentle rustle of the wind, the melody of birdsong. It's in these simple moments that life's true beauty resides. Embrace the warmth of a morning coffee, the laughter of loved ones, the comfort of a cozy blanket. Savor each sip, each laugh, each embrace.

Let gratitude fill your heart for the small joys that make life rich. In these moments, we find peace, contentment, and the reminder that life's greatest treasures are often found in life's simplest pleasures.

June 16

Letting Go of Control

Sometimes, life's a wild ride, right? We try to control every twist and turn, but it ain't easy. Let's take a breather, loosen those grip-tight fists, and let life do its thing. Trust me, it knows better than we do. It's like floating down a river – fighting the current only wears you out.

So, kick back, relax, and let the water carry you. Embrace the unknown, the unexpected. That's where the real magic happens. Surrender to the flow, and you'll find peace you never knew existed. Let's do this, together. We got this, even when we're letting go.

June 17

Resilience Amidst Challenges

Amidst life's chaos, know this: you're tougher than you think. Every challenge you face is a chance to grow, to stretch your limits, to learn what you're truly made of. It's okay to stumble, to feel overwhelmed, but don't let it define you. Your resilience, that's your superpower.

So, take a deep breath, gather your strength, and face whatever comes your way head-on. You've got this. Remember, it's not about avoiding the storms but learning to dance in the rain. With every setback, you're becoming stronger, wiser, and more capable than ever before. Keep pushing forward, warrior.

June 18

The Power of Forgiveness

In the depths of hurt, forgiveness isn't easy, but it's freeing. Letting go of resentment lifts a heavy burden off your shoulders. It's about you, not them. Forgiveness doesn't condone actions; it empowers you to reclaim your peace. It's a healing journey, messy and raw, but worth every tear shed.

You're not weak for forgiving; you're strong. Each step forward is a victory, a declaration of your resilience. So, embrace the discomfort, embrace the pain, and choose forgiveness. It's a radical act of self-love, a path to inner freedom, and a testament to your strength.

June 19

Cultivating Compassion

In life's whirlwind, it's easy to forget the power of compassion. Today, let's pause. Imagine walking in someone else's shoes, feeling their joy, their pain. It's about more than empathy; it's about connection. Maybe it's a smile to a stranger or a listening ear to a friend.

Compassion isn't just for others; it's a gift we give ourselves, softening our hearts, reminding us of our shared humanity. So, take a breath, let go of judgments, and embrace the messy, beautiful journey of understanding. In cultivating compassion, we create a ripple effect of love that heals both giver and receiver.

June 20

Finding Beauty in Brokenness

In a world that often feels broken, how do you find the beauty within yourself? It's not easy, but it starts with acceptance. Embrace every flaw, every scar, every imperfection, for they are a part of what makes you uniquely you.

Love yourself fiercely, not in spite of your brokenness, but because of it. Treat yourself with kindness, patience, and compassion. Allow yourself to heal, to grow, to bloom in the midst of adversity. Remember, it's okay to be a work in progress. You are worthy of love, from others and, most importantly, from yourself.

June 21

Embracing Self-Compassion

Just a little reminder for today to cut yourself some slack today. We're all human, after all! Embrace those imperfections and give yourself a big ol' hug. It's okay to stumble; it's how we learn to dance! So take a deep breath, let go of those expectations, and treat yourself with the kindness you deserve.

You're doing the best you can, and that's all anyone can ask for. Keep shining your light, even on the tough days. You're stronger than you know, and you've got a whole world of love and support behind you. Keep being kind to yourself, okay?

June 22

Choosing Kindness Every Day

You're busy, I'm busy, we're all just so busy these days and it's easy to get caught up in our own struggles, forgetting that everyone around us is fighting their battles too. Yet, amidst the chaos, there's a simple truth: kindness matters.

It's the gentle smile to a passing stranger, the helping hand to someone in need, the choice to respond with patience instead of frustration. It's not always easy; trust me, I've been there. But each day, we have the opportunity to choose kindness, to brighten someone's day, to spread a little love in this world. So let's make a pact: choose kindness every single day.

June 23

Faith Over Fear

So today's focus is all about faith over fear. Yeah, we all face those moments when fear creeps in, whispering doubts and worries. But guess what? You're not alone. Remember what 2 Timothy 1:7 says? "For God gave us a spirit not of fear but of power and love and self-control."

So, instead of letting fear hold you back, let it be a catalyst for faith. Step out boldly, knowing that with God on your side, you've got this. Embrace the journey, trust in His plan, and watch as fear fades in the light of your unwavering faith.

June 24

Honoring Your Journey

Today take a moment to honor your journey. Life' crazy ride, isn't it? It throws curveballs, but also serves up some sweet moments. Embrace both - the highs and the lows. When life gets tough, don't let it knock you out. Rise up stronger. Those rough patches?

They're lessons, not defeats. You're resilient, remember that. Each stumble is a chance to learn, grow, and become even more amazing. So, honor yourself today. Celebrate your victories, learn from your defeats, and keep moving forward with your head held high. Your journey is uniquely yours, so own it with pride.

June 25

Living Authentically Today

Okay so today let's get real, no masks, no pretending. Embrace who you are, flaws and all. It's liberating, trust me. So, wear your quirks proudly, laugh at your mistakes, and own your story. Let go of the need for approval and validation from others.

Your authenticity is your superpower. Be true to yourself, follow your heart, and live in alignment with your values. It's not always easy, but it's worth it. So, take a deep breath, embrace your uniqueness, and step into the world with confidence. You've got this!

June 26

Embracing Self-Discovery

Let's dig deep on today and discover what makes you tick. Take a moment to reflect on your passions, dreams, and quirks. Embrace every part of yourself—the good, the bad, and the downright messy.

It's in those moments of self-discovery that we truly grow and evolve. So, go ahead, lean into the unknown, explore new horizons, and don't be afraid to make mistakes along the way. Remember, it's all part of the journey towards becoming the best version of yourself. So, go ahead, dive in, and let the adventure of self-discovery begin!

June 27

Today's Gratitude Practice

Today is about practicing gratitude. Take a moment to breathe in deeply and appreciate the gift of another day. What's something small but mighty that brought a smile to your face? Maybe it's the warmth of the morning sun or the aroma of freshly brewed coffee.

Embrace those little moments of joy and let them fill your heart with gratitude. Remember, it's not about the grand gestures, but the tiny blessings that make life beautiful. So, here's to finding gratitude in the everyday moments and letting them light up your day!

June 28

Today's Courageous Step

Hey there, ready for a challenge? Today, break out of your comfort zone and take a leap of faith. It could be something small like striking up a conversation with a stranger or something bigger like pursuing a long-held dream. Whatever it is, muster up the courage within you and take that step forward. Remember, growth happens outside of our comfort zones. Embrace the discomfort and trust that amazing things lie on the other side. So, what courageous step will you take today?

The courageous step that I will take today will be to:

*Grab your journal and write down those courageous steps!

June 29

Cultivating Inner Peace

Finding inner peace can feel difficult at times especially when you have a million things going on. Here are three simple tips to light your way:

- ❖ Breathe Deeply: Take a moment to pause and breathe deeply. Inhale the present moment, exhale any tension, or worry.

- ❖ Pray & Practice Gratitude: Pray daily, seeking guidance and strength. Shift your focus to what's good in your life. Even in tough times, there's always something to be grateful for.

- ❖ Prioritize self-care: whether it's taking a walk-in nature, journaling, or enjoying a cup of tea.

Remember, peace isn't the absence of chaos, but rather the presence of calm within.

June 30

Love in Action Today

On the last day of this month, let me ask, when was the last time you told someone "I love you" and truly meant it? Heck, when was the last time you showed it and what did you do? If you can't remember, it's time to start practicing your love in action. Build up those love muscles today.

How can I build my love muscles? I'm glad you asked. Here are a few helpful tips:

- ❖ Start Small: Begin by expressing love through simple gestures, like sending a thoughtful text, cooking a meal, or offering a sincere compliment to yourself, a friend, a neighbor or loved one.

- ❖ Be Present: Show your love through active listening and being fully engaged in conversations. Demonstrate empathy and understanding towards others.

- ❖ Acts of Service: Look for opportunities to help others without expecting anything in return. Offer assistance, lend a hand, or support someone in need to show your love in action.

Love in action today, let's go

July

—

Stress Management and Resilience

July 1

Journey to Mental Wellness

At the start of this month, it's all about your journey to mental wellness. Some days might feel like you're trekking uphill, but trust me, you're making progress. It's okay to stumble; it's part of the climb. Remember to breathe through the tough spots and celebrate each little victory.

Take time to check in with yourself, to really listen to what your mind and body need. And when things feel heavy, know that it's alright to ask for help. You're not alone in this journey. Keep moving forward, one step at a time. You've got this, and brighter days are ahead.

July 2

Deep Breath, Stay Strong

When life throws you a curveball, it's easy to feel overwhelmed, but take a deep breath and remind yourself of your strength. You've overcome challenges before, and you can do it again. Trust in God, your own resilience and remember that tough times don't last forever.

Lean on your support system, take things one step at a time, and know that it's okay to ask for help when you need it. Stay grounded, stay strong, and know that you're capable of handling whatever comes your way. Let's go, you've got this today.

July 3

Mindful Moments

Take a breather today. Let's chat about those little moments that make a big difference. You know, those times when you pause, take a deep breath, and just soak it all in. Whether it's the warmth of the sun on your skin or the sound of laughter filling the air, these mindful moments are pure gold.

So, let's slow down, savor the sweetness of life, and find peace in the present. Remember, it's these simple moments that remind us of the beauty all around us. Take a moment today to be fully present and appreciate the magic of now.

July 4

Inner Peace Pathway

Navigating life's twists and turns can feel like a rollercoaster, right? But here's the kicker: just like a compass points north, we've got this inner guidance system leading us through the storms. Remember the scripture that talks about God's peace surpassing all understanding? Well, it's like finding a calm oasis in the midst of chaos.

So, when life throws curveballs, take a deep breath, trust that still, small voice within, and let that peace flow like a river. You're not alone on this journey; there's a divine roadmap guiding your steps, lighting up your path, even in the darkest of nights.

July 5

Finding Your Courage

Feeling a bit shaky lately? It's okay, we all do at times. Just remember, courage isn't about being fearless; it's about feeling the fear and doing it anyway. Take a deep breath, dig deep within yourself, and find that spark of bravery waiting to ignite.

It might be scary, but trust me, those amazing moments happen when you step outside your comfort zone. Embrace the unknown, embrace the journey, and most importantly, embrace yourself. Keep pushing forward, and before you know it, you'll be amazed at the heights you can reach.

July 6

Resilience Rising

In moments when life throws unexpected challenges, resilience becomes our strongest ally. Picture this: You've been tirelessly working towards a goal, pouring your heart and soul into it, only to face a setback that sends you reeling. Instead of succumbing to despair, you dig deep, summoning the resilience within.

You dust off your spirit, adjust your course, and forge ahead, stronger and wiser than before. Or imagine navigating through a turbulent phase in a relationship, where communication falters, and emotions run high. Instead of letting conflicts consume you, you choose patience, empathy, and understanding, fostering resilience to weather the storm together.

July 7

Calm Mind, Strong Soul

Ever wonder how some people stay so calm amidst chaos? Picture this: You're stuck in traffic, late for a meeting, and your phone keeps buzzing with urgent emails. Instead of succumbing to stress, take a deep breath. Close your eyes for a moment and remind yourself that you can handle this.

Focus on your breath, allowing each inhale and exhale to ground you. Remember, you're not defined by external circumstances; it's how you respond that matters. Embrace the power of a calm mind and a strong soul, knowing that you have the resilience to overcome any challenge that comes your way.

July 8

Grateful Heart, Steady Mind

Let's take a moment, right where you are. Breathe in deep, feel that? Your heart, beating strong. Yeah, life's tough, but guess what? So are you. Every hurdle you've cleared, every storm you've weathered, it's all made you into this resilient force.

I know sometimes it feels like the weight of the world's on your shoulders, but trust me, you're carrying it like a champ. So, when things get tough, remember this: gratitude steadies the mind, turns the chaos into calm. Today, let's count our blessings, find solace in the little things, and keep moving forward.

July 9

Shine Through Shadows

Amidst life's shadows, find your glow. Let your light pierce through darkness, illuminating paths for others. Embrace each challenge as a chance to grow, to evolve, to shine.

Remember, even the brightest stars flicker against the night sky. You're not alone in your struggles; they're just chapters in your story, shaping your journey. So, keep your head high, your heart open, and your spirit resilient. Let every setback be a setup for your comeback. Embrace your inner strength, for within you lies the power to radiate light and warmth, dispersing shadows wherever you go.

July 10

Embrace Your Strength

I'm over embracing my strength, now what? When you're drained and feel like there's nothing left, remember, God's got you. Even the strongest falter, but in weakness, His strength shines. Lean on Philippians 4:13, "I can do all things through Christ who strengthens me."

Let His power carry you when yours wanes. Take a breath, find solace in His presence, and embrace the strength He offers. You're not alone; He's with you in every trial. So, rest in His promise, rise in His might, and face each day knowing His grace is sufficient. You're stronger than you know, with His love as your unwavering support.

July 11

The Peaceful Seeker's Journey

On this journey, we seek peacefulness amidst life's whirlwinds. It's about finding peace in the chaos, trusting that divine grace guides us through every storm. Embrace each moment with faith, knowing that challenges are opportunities for growth.

When doubts creep in, let your soul whisper prayers of hope and strength. Remember, you're never alone on this path; God walks beside you, illuminating the way with His love. So, breathe deep, dear soul, and let His peace wash over you. In His presence, find the serenity that anchors your spirit and empowers you to face whatever lies ahead with unwavering faith.

July 12

Finding Light Within

In the midst of chaos, when the world feels heavy and your heart is aching, it's like stumbling around in the dark searching for a glimmer of light. It's tough, I get it. But here's the thing: even in the darkest of nights, there's a tiny spark within you waiting to ignite.

It's that resilient spirit, that flicker of hope, reminding you that you're stronger than you realize. So, take a deep breath, my friend. Close your eyes and feel for that warmth inside. That's your light. Nurture it, let it guide you through the darkness, and soon, you'll find your way back to brighter days.

July 13

Warrior Within You

Hey there, tough cookie! No matter the storm, don't forget the warrior within. Life throws a ton of situations at you, but you've got that fighting spirit deep down. You're not just a survivor; you're a warrior. Embrace those battle scars; they're proof of your strength. When the going gets tough, tap into that inner fighter.

You've faced challenges before and come out swinging. Keep pushing, keep believing, and keep fighting. You're more resilient than you think. So stand tall, chin up, and keep showing the world what a true warrior looks like. You've got this, and I'm cheering you on every step of the way!

July 14

Hope's Guiding Hand

Today, let's ride the waves of hope, navigating life's twists with a fearless spirit. Amidst the chaos, let hope be our guiding light, leading us through uncertainty with unwavering faith. When storms rage, remember, hope is not just a wish; it's a force that propels us forward.

Embrace it as your constant companion, whispering courage in moments of doubt. Let hope's gentle touch soothe your weary soul and ignite a fire within. In its glow, we find strength to face tomorrow, knowing that even in the darkest of nights, hope remains, lighting our path to brighter days ahead.

July 15

Trust Your Resilience

You have resilience in you, deep down where strength meets the soul. Trust it, even on the toughest days when the storm clouds gather. Remember, you've weathered many storms before and emerged stronger each time. Let that inner resilience guide you through life's twists and turns.

It's like a silent warrior within, ready to face whatever challenges come your way. Embrace it, lean into it, and watch how it carries you through. You're capable of more than you know, and your resilience is the anchor that keeps you steady amidst life's chaos. So, trust in yourself and your incredible resilience.

July 16

Daily Strength Dose

Today, let's dive into the depths of Psalm 46:1: "God is our refuge and strength, an ever-present help in trouble." In the hustle and bustle of life, we often forget that we have a source of unwavering strength within us.

Even in our most trying moments, God stands ready to be our refuge, our safe haven. Take a moment to breathe, to center yourself, and to remember that you are not alone. Draw upon the strength that resides within you, knowing that you are supported and guided by a divine presence that never wavers.

July 17

Rise Above Stress

Are you feeling overwhelmed? Take a breather, grab a cuppa, and let's chat. Stress is like that stubborn stain you can't seem to scrub away, but trust me, you've got the power to rise above it.

Try some deep breaths, maybe even a short walk, or blast your favorite tunes and dance it out. Remember, you're not alone in this. We all face stress, but it's how we deal with it that counts. So, take it one step at a time, focus on what you can control, and before you know it, you'll be soaring above that stress cloud.

July 18

Inner Peace Oasis

Find your inner peace oasis today. Picture this: a cozy nook, dimly lit by your favorite lamp. Sink into a plush chair, soft music in the background, a warm cup of tea in hand. Feel the tension melt away as you breathe deeply, embracing tranquility.

No rush, no noise, just you and your thoughts. Let worries drift away like clouds on a sunny day. This is your sanctuary, where calm reigns supreme. Let your mind wander, or simply be still. Find solace in this moment, knowing you're exactly where you need to be.

July 19

Breathe, Believe, Blossom

Inhale the calm, exhale the doubt. Trust in the rhythm of your breath, for with each exhale, release the weight you carry. Believe in the strength within you, waiting to blossom. Embrace the stillness of this moment, knowing that within you lies the power to rise.

Let your breath be your anchor, grounding you in the present. Feel the gentle rhythm of your heartbeat, a reminder of your resilience. As you breathe in, invite in peace; as you breathe out, let go of worry. In this simple act of breathing, find solace, find strength, and let your spirit bloom.

July 20

Grounded Spirit, Soaring Soul

Find solace in your faith today, where grounded roots meet the sky. Let your spirit soar above doubts and fears, anchored in the certainty of divine love. Each day, breathe in courage, exhale worries, and trust in the path set before you. You're not alone on this journey; divine hands guide your steps, whispering promises of hope and strength.

Embrace each moment with gratitude, for even amidst challenges, your soul finds wings to rise. Let faith be your compass, leading you to the calm waters of peace, where your grounded spirit meets the heavens, and your soul finds its true home.

July 21

Heart's Resilience Rhythm

Feel your heartbeat? It's like your own rhythm, steady and strong, even with all you have going on. Just like a song, your heart sings a melody of resilience, beating with every challenge, every triumph. Sometimes it races, like when excitement fills your soul. Other times, it slows, calming you down in moments of chaos.

That beat? It's proof of your strength, your resilience. It's the drumbeat of your journey, guiding you through highs and lows. So, when life tests you, listen to that rhythm, feel its power, and know that you've got what it takes to keep dancing through it all.

July 22

Courageous Steps Forward

Today, let's imagine ourselves stepping into uncharted territory, where courage is our compass and faith our guide. Picture taking those first brave steps, feeling the ground beneath your feet, each stride a testament to your resilience. Embrace the unknown with an open heart, knowing that every step forward is a victory, regardless of the outcome.

Trust in your inner strength and the wisdom of your soul as you navigate this new path. Remember, it's okay to feel uncertain; it's part of the journey. But with each courageous step, you're paving the way for a brighter, more fulfilling tomorrow. Keep moving forward.

July 23

Tranquil Mindset Melodies

Feelin' those peaceful vibes today? Picture this: you're sippin' on a cold lemonade or a warm cup of tea, cozy in your fave spot, tunes playin' softly in the background. It's like your mind's takin' a sweet vacation, no stress allowed. Let those worries drift away like clouds on a sunny day.

Embrace that tranquility friend, let it seep into every part of your being. Feel the rhythm of your heartbeat slowin' down, syncin' with the calm of the moment. Let this peaceful melody be your soundtrack, playin' on repeat in your soul. Peace isn't just a place, it's a state of mind, and you're livin' it.

MINNINA M. SMITH
July 24

Empowered Mind, Stronger You

Let's chew on this for a sec: remember that scripture, "Let this mind be in you, which was also in Christ Jesus"? It's like a reminder to tap into that inner strength, that resilient mindset. When life throws its curveballs, you gotta pull from that Christ-like resilience, you know?

Let your mind be your shield against stress, your anchor in the storm. Believe me, you've got this. Embrace that empowered mindset, and watch yourself grow stronger, more resilient every day. Rock your journey with the kind of mindset that moves mountains and conquers challenges. You're unstoppable, my friend.

July 25

Spark of Resilience

You know that movie, "300," where they shout "This is Sparta!"? Well, life's a bit like that. Sometimes, you've gotta ignite that warrior spirit. When challenges hit hard, it's not about backing down. It's about standing tall, planting your feet, and saying, "This is me, and I'm not backing down." That's the spark of resilience, that fiery determination inside you.

It's about finding strength in the face of adversity, refusing to let life's storms dim your light. So, when life throws its curveballs, remember: you've got that spark within you. Let it ignite your resilience and fuel your journey.

MINNINA M. SMITH
July 26

Radiate Inner Calm

In the tranquil halls of ancient monasteries, monks practice a sacred art: the mastery of calm. Picture this: amidst their daily tasks, they pause, inhaling serenity and exhaling stress. They find solace in the rhythm of their breath, grounding themselves in the present moment.

As they navigate life's storms, they remain steady, like a sturdy tree swaying in the breeze. Their secret? A deep connection to their inner selves, nurturing their spirits with peace. It reminds me of Psalm 46:10, "Be still, and know that I am God." Today, let's follow their lead and radiate that inner calm.

July 27

Trails of Mindfulness

Today, find your stride on the trails of mindfulness. Listen to the rhythm of your breath, syncopating with each step, grounding you in the present moment. Feel the earth beneath your feet, connecting you to the essence of existence. Let your worries fade like footprints in the sand, as you wander through the wilderness of your thoughts.

Embrace the stillness of nature's symphony, where the chirping of birds and rustling of leaves become your guiding melody. On these trails, discover the peace that comes from simply being, and let mindfulness pave the way to your soul's sanctuary.

July 28

Warrior's Wisdom Words

Let's imagine an old veteran Soldier giving you wisdom, this is what they would say: Hey there, newbie. Listen up. I've been where you are, walked the same dirt, felt the same heat. But here's the deal – you're stronger than you think. You got grit, resilience deep in your bones. When it feels like you're at your limit, push a little harder.

When the road gets tough, find that inner warrior. Trust me, there's a hero in you waiting to emerge. So, chin up, chest out, and keep marching forward. You're not alone in this journey. We're all warriors in our own right, fighting side by side.

July 29

God: Your Guiding Light

In this wild world, it's easy to lose your way, isn't it? But guess what? You aren't alone. Nope, not by a long shot. Take a sec, close your eyes, and feel that spark within you? Yeah, that's your North Star, your guiding light, leading you through every twist and turn.

So, when you're feeling lost or overwhelmed, just remember, you've got a direct line to the Big Guy up there. Trust in that light, follow its glow, and you'll find your path, one step at a time. You got this, and you aren't ever alone in this crazy ride.

July 30

Grounded in Gratitude

Did you tell God thanks today? Not for the grand gestures, but the simple stuff. The sun's warmth, a laugh shared, a cool breeze, your family & friends. Gratitude's like a secret key, unlocking joy in everyday moments.

It's easy to forget, lost in the swirl of our days. But take a moment, breathe it in. Thank Him for the small blessings, the unnoticed mercies. They add up, you know? Grounds us, reminds us of His constant love. So, before you start your day or hit the hay tonight, whisper that 'thank you'. Trust me, it'll brighten your day, inside and out.

July 31

Embracing Summer's Splendor

Today, soak up the sunshine and let its warmth fill your soul. Take a moment to appreciate the beauty around you, from the vibrant flowers to the gentle breeze. Remember, life is a precious gift, and every moment is an opportunity to find joy and gratitude.

As July comes to a close, reflect on the memories you've made and the blessings you've received. Let go of any worries or stresses, and simply bask in the summer's splendor. Trust that brighter days are ahead, and embrace the warmth of the season with an open heart.

MINNINA M. SMITH

August

—

Fitness and Exercise Goals

August 1

Morning Miles

I hope you're staying with it, embracing those morning miles like a trusted companion on your journey. Every step you take isn't just about exercise; it's a declaration of self-love and commitment to your well-being. As you lace up those sneakers and hit the pavement, feel the rhythm of your heartbeat syncing with the rhythm of life itself.

These morning miles aren't just about physical fitness; they're about nurturing your soul, finding clarity in the quiet, and setting the tone for a day filled with positivity and purpose. Keep putting one foot in front of the other, knowing each step brings you closer to your best self.

August 2

Sweat Sessions

Today, let's dive into some serious sweat sessions! Sure, the couch might seem tempting, but trust me, your body and mind will thank you later. It's not just about looking good; it's about feeling good from the inside out. So, lace up those sneakers, crank up the tunes, and let's get moving!

Whether it's a brisk walk, a heart-pumping HIIT session, or some mindful yoga, every drop of sweat is a step towards a healthier, happier you. So, let's break a sweat, shake off those worries, and embrace the power of movement in our daily lives!

August 3

Mindful Movement

In the rhythm of life, it's the little steps that add up to big victories. Each stretch, each bend, every flex and sway, they're not just motions; they're mini miracles, guiding us forward on our journey. When we lace up those sneakers or roll out that yoga mat, it's not just about the sweat; it's about the soul.

With each mindful movement, we're not just toning muscles; we're strengthening resolve. So let's dance to the beat of our own drum, embracing every twist and turn, knowing that with each step, we're one step closer to our best selves.

August 4

Fitness Fuel

You know that dress you've been eyeing? Well, picture rocking it with confidence, feeling energized and strong! And fellas, imagine crushing your workout goals, pushing past limits you never thought possible. That's the power of fitness fuel! It's not just about sweating it out; it's about embracing your potential, feeling unstoppable, and owning every moment.

So, lace up those sneakers or grab those weights – let's ignite that fire within, fueling our bodies and minds to conquer anything that comes our way. Together, we're unstoppable on this journey to fitness and fulfillment!

August 5

Stronger Every Step

Just wanted to remind you that you're doing great. Life's a journey, and every step you take, you're getting stronger. Even when things get tough, remember that each hurdle you overcome makes you tougher. It's okay to stumble sometimes; it's part of the process.

Just keep moving forward, and you'll see how resilient you truly are. You've got this! Keep believing in yourself and your ability to overcome any challenge. With each step, you're becoming stronger, wiser, and more resilient. So keep going, one step at a time, and remember that you're never alone in this journey.

August 6

Empowered Exercise

In this journey of faith and fitness, each step is a testament to our inner strength. Let's lace up our shoes, hit the pavement, and feel the rhythm of our hearts beating in sync with our Creator's love. As we lift weights, let's also lift our spirits, knowing that God's power is within us, pushing us to reach new heights.

With every squat and stretch, let's thank Him for the gift of movement and the opportunity to honor our bodies. In this journey of empowered exercise, let's lean on His grace, trusting that He strengthens us not just physically, but spiritually too.

August 7

Fitness Focus

It's all about fitness this month! It's about finding what moves you, both physically and mentally. Whether it's a jog in the park, hitting the gym, or even a dance party in your living room, let's get those endorphins flowing! Remember, it's not just about the workout; it's about how it makes you feel.

So, sweat it out, push yourself a little more each day, and celebrate those small victories. Your health matters, and every step you take towards your fitness goals is a step towards a happier, healthier you. You've got this!

August 8

Mind Over Matter

I know this journey can feel like an uphill battle sometimes. There'll be days when getting out of bed feels like climbing Everest. But remember, it's all about mind over matter. Push past those mental barriers, even when your body wants to quit.

You've got this! Whether it's hitting the gym or just going for a walk, every step counts. And trust me, once you get going, you'll feel unstoppable. So lace up those shoes, put on your favorite playlist, and let's conquer those fitness goals together. Remember, the hardest part is often taking that first step.

August 9

Body Boost

Today remember to start your day with fuel that powers you forward—whole grains, fruits, and protein-packed breakfasts set the tone. End on a satisfying note with greens, lean proteins, and healthy fats. These choices aren't just about calories; they're about giving your body the right tools to thrive.

It's not about restrictions but about feeling energized, strong, and ready for whatever life throws your way. Every meal is an opportunity to nourish your body and soul, to remind yourself that you're worth the effort. So, indulge in foods that make you feel good and keep that body boost going from sunrise to sunset.

August 10

Mind-Body Movement

Remind yourself that your fitness journey is not just about pumping iron or sweating buckets – it's about nurturing your whole self. When you move your body, whether it's a brisk walk or dancing in your living room, you're not just toning muscles; you're lifting your spirits and refreshing your mind.

It's like giving your soul a much-needed hug. So, when you're feeling a bit low or stressed, remember that even a short walk or a few stretches can work wonders. Trust me, your body and soul will thank you for it. Let's keep moving and grooving together!

August 11

Fit and Focused

"Let's get physical, physical" - That song just makes me want to lace up my sneakers and hit the pavement! But seriously, finding that focus on fitness is like finding a beat to dance to; it gets you moving, it gets you grooving, and it makes you feel alive.

So let's sweat it out, not just for the physical gains but for the mental clarity it brings. Remember, each step you take is a step toward a stronger, healthier you. So, let's stay fit, stay focused, and keep moving forward, one workout at a time.

August 12

Daily Drive

Hey there! How's your day going? Just wanted to remind you to keep up that daily drive, even if it feels tough. I know sometimes it's hard to find the motivation, but trust me, every little step counts.

Whether it's a quick walk around the block or a full-blown workout, it's all about taking care of yourself. And you deserve that. So, take a deep breath, put on those sneakers, and let's tackle this together. You've got this, and I'm cheering you on every step of the way.

August 13

Mindful Motion

Today, let's hustle for that muscle! Strap on those sneakers, grab your water bottle, and let's give those weights a lift like they owe us money! Remember, sweating is just your fat crying because it knows it's leaving you. So, let's turn up the music, dance like nobody's watching (even if they are), and make our hearts race like they're in a marathon.

Embrace the burn, because that's where the magic happens. And hey, if you need a little extra motivation, just imagine the post-workout snack waiting for you at the finish line. Let's crush those fitness goals, one rep at a time!

August 14

Wellness Walks

Oh the wonderfulness of wellness; it's a journey. Lace up those sneakers, step outside, and breathe in the fresh air. Each stride is a step toward mental clarity and spiritual renewal. Let the rhythm of your steps sync with the beat of your heart as you embark on your wellness walk.

With each footfall, feel the weight of your worries lift, replaced by a sense of peace and purpose. Know that you're not alone on this path; the divine presence walks beside you, guiding your steps and illuminating the path ahead. Embrace the journey, one step at a time, let's go.

August 15

Fitness Flow

Are you ready to get motivated today? Let's talk about getting into that fitness flow! It's not just about physical gains; it's about the mental lift too. When you're out there, sweating it out, it's like a dance with life itself. Each step, each breath, is a prayer for strength and resilience.

So lace up those shoes again, turn up the tunes, and let's flow through this workout like it's a celebration of life. Feel the energy coursing through you, reminding you that you're capable of anything, inside and out. Let's move and groove, embracing the journey ahead!

August 16

Soulful Sweat

How about trying something new? How about dancing? You don't have to be a pro, just move your body and let the rhythm take over. It's not just about burning calories; it's about letting your soul shine through movement.

Whether it's a solo dance party in your living room or joining a class, embrace the joy of moving to music. Let go of any self-consciousness and focus on how good it feels to be alive, to be able to dance. Trust me, your body and mind will thank you for it. Let's sweat it out and feel the soulful vibes.

August 17

Mental Muscle

Have you been feeling a bit overwhelmed lately? It's okay, we all hit those rough patches. Just remember, mental strength is just as important as physical fitness. Take some time today to flex your "mental muscle." That might mean meditating, journaling, or just taking a moment to breathe deeply.

You've got this! Every small step you take towards caring for your mental health is a victory. So, whether you're hitting the gym or taking a mental health day, know that you're building resilience and strength from the inside out. Keep going, friend!

August 18

Strength in Stillness

Today take a breath, feel the earth beneath your feet, and let your worries slip away. It's okay to pause, to reflect, to recharge. Strength isn't always about moving forward; sometimes, it's about finding peace in the present. Embrace the quiet moments, for they are where true resilience grows.

Allow yourself to just be, to let your mind wander and your soul breathe. In the stillness, you'll discover a strength you never knew you had—the power to face whatever comes your way with grace and resilience.

August 19

Fitness Freedom

Today's all about giving yourself that well-deserved break. Let your body soak up the rest like a sponge in a hot tub. It's not just about physical recovery; it's also a mental reset. So, chill out, catch up on your favorite show, or maybe take a leisurely stroll.

Whatever floats your boat, do it guilt-free. Remember, rest days are just as crucial as those workout sessions. They're like the secret sauce that keeps you going strong. So, kick back, relax, and recharge those batteries. Tomorrow, you'll be ready to hit the ground running, feeling fresher than ever!

August 20

Body Balance

Let's find our body balance. Start with stretching, reaching for the sky, and feeling the earth beneath your feet. Tune into your breath, letting it guide your movements. Remember, it's not just about the sweat, but the soulful connection to your body.

Find joy in the motion, whether it's a dance or a gentle walk. Embrace the journey, honoring your body's strength and resilience. Don't forget to hydrate, nourish, and rest. You're not just working out; you're nurturing your soul. Keep moving, keep breathing, and keep listening to your body's wisdom. You've got this!

August 21

Mindful Muscles

Today make it about tuning into your muscles. Picture this: every move you make, every step you take, it's all a step towards your wellness goals. Let's infuse our workouts with mindfulness, feeling every stretch and every rep.

Your muscles aren't just growing physically; they're growing stronger mentally too. So lace up those sneakers, crank up the tunes, and let's hustle our way to a healthier, happier you!

August 22

Wellness Walks

Let's chat about something awesome – walking! Yep, that simple stroll counts as exercise too. After a hectic day, taking a walk can be a game-changer. It's like hitting the reset button for your mind. The rhythm of your steps, the fresh air, it's all good stuff.

Plus, it's a chance to soak in some nature and let go of all that stress. So, lace up those shoes, step outside, and let your worries melt away with each stride. Remember, taking care of your mind is just as important as taking care of your body. Walk on, friend!

August 23

Inner Strength

Today, let's talk about a different kind of fitness: your inner strength. It's not just about pumping iron or running marathons; it's about the strength that comes from within, from your spirit. As Philippians 4:13 says, "I can do all things through Christ who strengthens me."

So, when you're feeling tired or discouraged on your fitness journey, remember that you have a source of strength that goes beyond what you can see or feel. Tap into that inner strength, believe in yourself, and keep pushing forward. You've got this!

August 24

Keep That Body Moving Friend

Hey there! You know what's better than a one-hour workout? A two-hour nap! Just kidding, but seriously, let's lace up those sneakers once again and get moving. Whether it's a power walk, yoga session, or dancing in the living room, let's keep that body grooving.

Remember, we're not just building physical strength; we're nurturing our spirit too. So, let's sweat out the stress and lift our spirits high. You've got this, and with a little faith and a lot of movement, we're unstoppable. Here's to joyful jumps, spirited stretches, and a heart that's as light as our laughter. Let's move, shake, and praise!

August 25

Body Bliss

Body Bliss is that feeling of pure contentment and joy that washes over you after a great workout. It's the satisfaction of knowing you've taken a step toward your fitness and exercise goals.

Whether it's a brisk walk in the park, a challenging yoga session, or hitting the weights at the gym, each movement brings you closer to your best self. Soak in the endorphins, revel in the strength of your body, and embrace the journey to becoming the healthiest, happiest version of yourself. Remember, every step, every rep, and every drop of sweat is a victory worth celebrating.

August 26

Fitness Fusion

Hey there, ready to blend some fitness fun into your day? Let's sweat it out, shake off those worries, and groove to the rhythm of your body. It's not just about reps and sets; it's about feeling alive, strong, and unstoppable. Whether it's a dance session in the living room or a jog around the block, make fitness your favorite fusion of joy and strength. You already know what I'm going to say, so go ahead and lace up those sneakers, crank up the tunes, and let the endorphins flow.

Remember, every step, jump, and stretch brings us closer to a healthier, happier version of ourselves. Rock this fitness fusion!

August 27

Morning Momentum

Rise and shine, beautiful soul! Today's your day to conquer those fitness goals with a smile. Remember, every step is a victory, every breath a blessing. Embrace the sunshine, feel the breeze on your face, and let God's love fill your spirit as you move.

Whether it's a brisk walk, a joyful jog, or a dance around the living room, let's make it count. With each movement, you're not just sculpting your body; you're nurturing your soul. So, let's kick off this day with energy, enthusiasm, and faith!

August 28

Strength in Stride

Hey there, superstar! Can you believe you're about to wrap up another month soon? Take a moment to pat yourself on the back because you've come a long way. Remember those fitness goals we set at the beginning? Well, look at you now, striding stronger and feeling more alive with every step.

It's incredible what a little determination and a whole lot of faith can do, isn't it? So here's to celebrating your progress, your resilience, and your unwavering spirit. Keep pushing forward, keep believing, and keep shining bright. You're unstoppable, and I can't wait to see what amazing feats you conquer next!

August 29

Strengthening the Soul Through Movement

Today, let's celebrate the wonder of our bodies and the joy of movement. Each step, each stretch, is a testament to our resilience and vitality. As we embark on our fitness journey, let's remember that every moment of activity is an opportunity to connect with our inner strength and embrace the gift of health.

August 30

Finding Peace in Active Pursuits

Amidst the hustle and bustle of life, let's find solace in our active pursuits. Whether it's a brisk walk in nature or a challenging workout session, let's allow movement to be our sanctuary.

As we engage our bodies, let's also quiet our minds and invite peace to dwell within us.

August 31

Celebrating Victories, Big and Small

As the month comes to a close, let's take a moment to celebrate our victories, big and small. Whether it's reaching a fitness milestone or simply showing up for ourselves each day, every achievement deserves recognition.

Let's carry this spirit of celebration into the days ahead, knowing that with dedication and perseverance, we can continue to reach new heights on our fitness journey.

MINNINA M. SMITH

September

—

Self-Mental Health Awareness

September 1

Overcoming Anxiety

Let's get into the depths of our souls and address the anxiety that grips us. It's okay to feel overwhelmed, but remember, you're not alone. Turn to your faith, knowing that God's strength is greater than your fears. Take each moment as it comes, breathing in His peace and exhaling the worries that burden your heart.

Trust in His plan for you, knowing that every challenge you face is an opportunity for growth. Lean on His promises, for He has promised to never leave you nor forsake you. With faith as your anchor, you can overcome anxiety and find serenity in His embrace.

September 2

Coping with Stress

How do you cope with stress? It can be a journey that tests your faith and resilience. In these moments, find solace in knowing you're not alone. Turn to prayer, meditation, or a supportive community. Trust that God's grace sustains you, offering strength in our weakest moments.

Embrace vulnerability, allowing yourself to feel the weight of your emotions. Remember, it's okay to seek help when needed. Through faith, we find hope amidst chaos, and through perseverance, we emerge stronger. Keep holding on, knowing that brighter days are ahead, and God's love is ever-present in our struggles.

September 3

Embracing Imperfection

Life isn't about being flawless; it's about embracing our imperfections. It's in our flaws that we find our uniqueness, our humanity. Each scar, each mistake, tells a story of resilience and growth. So, let's stop striving for perfection and start celebrating our imperfections. They make us who we are. They remind us that we're all a work in progress, and that's okay. Embrace your quirks, your vulnerabilities, your mistakes.

They are what make you beautifully imperfect. And remember, it's not about being perfect; it's about being perfectly you. So, let's embrace imperfection and live authentically, flaws and all.

September 4

Nurturing Self-Love

In moments of doubt, remember your worth. Self-love isn't always easy; it's a journey of acceptance and forgiveness. Embrace your flaws; they make you unique. Be gentle with yourself, just as you would with a cherished friend. Recognize the beauty within you, flaws and all. Allow yourself grace when you stumble; it's part of the human experience.

You're worthy of love, kindness, and respect, from both yourself and others. Take time to care for your mind, body, and soul. Nurture your inner self with positive thoughts, self-care rituals, and meaningful connections. Today, choose to love yourself a little more.

MINNINA M. SMITH
September 5

Forgiving Yourself

We all carry burdens, mistakes made, roads not taken. Yet, forgiveness starts within. Accepting our flaws, our humanity, leads to liberation. Each stumble is a lesson, each failure a step toward growth. Release the weight of self-blame, for it stifles progress.

Embrace self-compassion; it's a journey, not a destination. Remember, to err is human; to forgive, divine. Grant yourself the grace you readily offer others. In forgiving yourself, you grant permission to evolve, to rewrite your narrative. Today, shed the shackles of regret; embrace the freedom of forgiveness. For in forgiving yourself, you open the door to true self-discovery and healing.

September 6

Overcoming Obstacles

Remember that life presents hurdles we must overcome. Each obstacle, though daunting, offers an opportunity for growth. It's natural to feel overwhelmed, but remember, you possess the strength to persevere. Embrace challenges as stepping stones, not barriers.

Acknowledge your fears and doubts, but don't let them define you. Seek support when needed; you're not alone in this journey. Every setback is a chance to learn, adapt, and emerge stronger. Trust in your resilience and inner wisdom. Embrace the process, knowing that each obstacle conquered brings you closer to the person you're meant to be. You've got this.

September 7

Cultivating Resilience

Today's reminder is that it's okay to feel overwhelmed, to stumble, and to question. But remember, faith isn't about being fearless; it's about finding courage in the face of fear. It's about knowing that even in our weakest moments, we're held by a strength greater than ourselves.

So, embrace the journey with all its twists and turns, knowing that each setback is an opportunity for growth, each challenge a chance to build resilience. With unwavering faith and a heart open to grace, you'll find the strength to weather any storm and emerge stronger, wiser, and more resilient than ever before.

September 8

Celebrating Progress

I want you to take a moment to reflect on how far you've come. Each step forward, no matter how small, is worth celebrating. Remember, progress isn't always linear, and setbacks are a natural part of growth. Embrace your journey with compassion and acknowledge the effort you've put in. Even on challenging days, recognize the resilience within you. You're stronger than you realize.

Trust in your ability to overcome obstacles and keep moving forward. Your progress, no matter how gradual, is a testament to your strength and determination. Take pride in how far you've come, and keep pressing on with courage and hope.

September 9

Letting Go

Let it go today. I know it's easier said than done. Trust me, I've been there. Sometimes holding onto things only weighs us down. It could be past mistakes, grudges, or even expectations. But as tough as it may seem, releasing those burdens can bring a sense of freedom.

It's about making space for new beginnings, opportunities, and growth. So take a deep breath, acknowledge what's weighing you down, and slowly release it. Remember, it's a process, and it's okay to take it one step at a time. You've got this.

September 10

Renewed Strength

You might be feeling tired, worn out, or uncertain about what lies ahead. But in these moments, remember this: strength is not just about physical power; it's about resilience, determination, and the courage to keep going, even when it feels impossible.

Each day brings new opportunities for growth and renewal. Embrace the challenges as chances to become stronger. Trust in your ability to overcome obstacles and know that you're not alone in this journey. You have within you the power to rise above any circumstance and emerge with renewed strength and purpose. Keep moving forward, one step at a time.

September 11

Gratitude Practice

Gratitude, it's not always easy, especially when life throws us curveballs. But even in the midst of challenges, there's always something to be thankful for. It could be a simple sunrise, a warm cup of coffee, or the smile of a loved one. Gratitude isn't just about saying thank you; it's about recognizing the blessings, big and small, that we're given each day.

It's about shifting our focus from what's going wrong to what's going right. So today, let's take a moment to count our blessings and thank God for His faithfulness in every season of life.

September 12

Embracing Vulnerability

Let's talk about vulnerability. It's not weakness; it's courage in its rawest form. Vulnerability means allowing yourself to be seen, flaws and all, without the armor of pretense. It's opening up, sharing your fears, doubts, and struggles, knowing that it's okay not to have it all together.

When we embrace vulnerability, we invite genuine connections, empathy, and growth into our lives. It's about authenticity, owning our stories, and finding strength in our vulnerabilities. So, let's embrace vulnerability today, knowing that it's the birthplace of love, belonging, and true authenticity.

September 13

Connecting with Others

In life, connecting with others is both a challenge and a blessing. It's about vulnerability, trust, and sometimes, taking risks. But within those connections lie the potential for growth, understanding, and love. It's okay to feel apprehensive or unsure; that's part of the journey.

Just remember, every connection, whether brief or enduring, shapes our lives in profound ways. So, reach out, listen, and be present. Share your story and allow others to share theirs. In those moments of genuine connection, we find solace, strength, and the beauty of our shared humanity.

September 14

Accepting Challenges

Life is a journey of challenges, some unexpected, others anticipated. Embracing these challenges is daunting, but within them lies growth and strength. It's okay to feel overwhelmed or uncertain; that's part of the process. Remember, each challenge is an opportunity for growth, a chance to learn, and a step toward your dreams.

Lean into discomfort, for it's where resilience is forged. Trust yourself and your abilities; you've overcome challenges before, and you'll do it again. With each hurdle, you become stronger, wiser, and more capable. Embrace the challenges before you; they're shaping you into the person you're destined to be.

September 15

Building Confidence

Confidence. You know, that inner spark that lights you up and makes you feel like you can conquer the world? Yeah, that's what we're diving into today. So, here's the deal: you've got this incredible potential inside you, just waiting to shine. It's all about embracing who you are, flaws and all, and owning it.

Take those small steps, celebrate your victories (no matter how tiny), and trust yourself along the way. You're stronger than you think, and the world needs your unique brilliance. So go ahead, rock that confidence like a boss!

September 16

Respecting Your Limits

Remember it's okay to set boundaries and respect your limits. You're not invincible, and that's perfectly fine. Listen to your body and mind, they're trying to tell you something important. Pushing yourself too hard won't do any good in the long run. Take breaks when needed, recharge your batteries, and come back stronger.

Your well-being matters, so prioritize it. It's not about being selfish, it's about self-care. Give yourself permission to say no and prioritize your needs. Remember, you're worthy of respect, especially from yourself. So, take a breath, set those boundaries, and honor your limits.

September 17

Setting Realistic Goals

Today's all about setting those goals, but let's keep it real, okay? Think about what you want to achieve, but also consider what's actually doable. Don't overwhelm yourself with unrealistic expectations.

Break it down into smaller steps, and celebrate each little win along the way. Remember, progress is progress, no matter how small. You got this! So, let's set those goals, crush them one step at a time, and watch how they add up to something amazing. Just keep pushing forward, and remember to be kind to yourself along the journey. You're doing great!

September 18

Fostering Healthy Relationships

Let's chat about relationships today. It's all about finding your tribe, you know? Surround yourself with those who lift you up, who understand your quirks, and who make you feel valued. But hey, it's a two-way street! Be the kind of friend you want to have.

Listen, support, and show up when it matters. And don't forget, it's okay to set boundaries too. Your mental health matters, and it starts with the company you keep. So, here's to fostering those healthy connections and creating a tribe that feels like home. You've got this!

September 19

Celebrating Recovery

Today let's celebrate the journey of recovery, if not yours then the journey of another! It's not always easy, but every step forward is worth acknowledging. Remember those moments when you felt like giving up?

Well, you didn't, and look how far you've come! Your strength and resilience are truly inspiring. So, take a moment to pat yourself on the back, you've earned it. And if you're still struggling, that's okay too. Just know that you're not alone, and there's always hope for brighter days ahead. Keep pushing forward, one day at a time. You've got this!

September 20

Managing Depression

Navigating through the fog, depression isn't just feeling down, it's like being trapped in a dark tunnel with no light at the end. It's the weight on your chest, the voice in your head telling you you're not good enough. But guess what? You're not alone.

There's a way out, a path to brighter days. It's about taking it one step at a time, reaching out for help, finding what brings even a sliver of light into your world. It's okay to not be okay, but it's also okay to seek support and find your way back to the sunshine.

September 21

Healing Trauma

Navigating life's rough patches, healing trauma is about acknowledging and addressing emotional wounds. It's the process of finding solace in our journey, recognizing the scars that shape us. While it's often misunderstood, depression is more than just feeling sad; it's a heavy weight, a constant struggle.

Yet, through therapy, self-care, and support, we learn to carry this burden with grace. Healing takes time, patience, and vulnerability. It's about allowing ourselves to feel, to heal, and to grow. As we embrace our journey, we find strength in our scars, and gradually, we discover the beauty in our brokenness.

September 22

Managing Anger

Anger, a powerful but often misunderstood emotion, is our body's natural response to threats or injustice. It's okay to feel angry, but it's crucial to understand why. Maybe it's a signal that boundaries were crossed or a situation feels unjust.

By acknowledging anger, we take the first step in managing it. Through deep breaths, introspection, and sometimes seeking help, we can tame the flames. Remember, anger is like a fire—it can warm us or burn us. Let's learn to wield it wisely, harnessing its energy for positive change.

September 23

Overcoming Fear

In the face of fear, remember this: you're never alone. Even in the darkest moments, there's a guiding light, a presence that whispers, "You are loved, you are protected."

Trust in something greater than yourself, whether it's the universe, God, or the energy of love itself. Embrace faith, not in the absence of fear, but in spite of it. Let your faith be stronger than your fear, guiding you forward, one step at a time. Know that you're capable, you're resilient, and you're worthy of every blessing that awaits on the other side of fear.

September 24

Prioritizing Self-Reflection

In those quiet moments, take time to ponder, not just the words spoken, but the whispers of your soul. It's in these reflections that we find clarity, guidance, and peace. Trust in the divine presence that gently nudges you towards self-discovery. Embrace the journey of understanding yourself better, for in doing so, you open doors to growth and transformation.

Let faith be your anchor, guiding you through the waves of uncertainty. Remember, it's okay to pause, to breathe, to seek solace in the arms of grace. May each moment of self-reflection bring you closer to the light within.

September 25

Building Self-Esteem

In this life, remember you're a masterpiece, crafted by the hands of the divine. You're unique, with strengths and beauty that only you possess. So, when those doubts creep in, when you question your worth, take a moment to pause.

Look within and see the light that shines from your soul. You're here for a reason, with a purpose that's waiting to be embraced. Let go of comparison, of the need for validation from others. Stand tall, knowing that you are loved, valued, and cherished by the One who created you. Embrace your worth, and let your light shine bright.

September 26

Overcoming Self-Doubt

You know those days when doubt creeps in and clouds your mind? Yeah, we've all been there. But here's the thing, you're stronger than you think. Take a moment, breathe, and remind yourself of your worth. Believe that you're capable of achieving great things.

Trust in a higher power that guides you, even when the path seems uncertain. Embrace faith over fear, knowing that you're not alone in this journey. Each step forward, no matter how small, is a victory worth celebrating. So, keep going, my friend. God's got you and you've got this.

September 27

Honoring Your Emotions

In life's rollercoaster, emotions are our raw, unfiltered compasses. They guide us through the highs and lows, teaching us invaluable lessons about ourselves. So, honor them. Allow yourself to feel deeply, whether it's joy, sorrow, or everything in between.

Each emotion is a thread in the fabric of your soul, weaving a tapestry of experiences that shape who you are. Trust that even in the darkest moments, there's a glimmer of divine light, guiding you towards healing and growth. Embrace the journey, knowing that every tear shed and every smile shared is a testament to the resilience of your spirit.

September 28

Cultivating Patience

Hang tight, beautiful soul! Life can be hard sometimes, but patience is your superpower. Remember, good things take time to unfold. Embrace the waiting game with a smile, knowing that every delay brings you closer to your dreams.

Remember to take a deep breath, trust the process, and enjoy the journey. While you wait, sprinkle some kindness, dance in the rain, and savor life's little joys. Let patience be your guide, leading you to moments of serenity and unexpected blessings. So, chin up, heart open, and keep blooming at your own pace. The best is yet to come, and it's worth every second.

September 29

Seeking Balance

Take a pause today, close your eyes, and just breathe. Inhale the calm, exhale the chaos. Let your mind wander freely, embracing the stillness within. It's not about escaping reality; it's about finding your center amidst the storm. With each breath, release tension, find clarity, and reconnect with yourself.

Let the rhythm of your breath guide you to a place of peace and serenity. In this moment of stillness, you'll discover the balance you've been seeking, anchoring yourself in the present and opening your heart to the beauty of each passing moment.

September 30

Embracing Healing and Hope

As you bid farewell to September, reflect on your journey of healing and hope you've embarked upon this month. In the midst of life's storms, remember Psalm 34:18, "The Lord is close to the brokenhearted and saves those who are crushed in spirit." Through our struggles, God is ever-present, offering comfort and restoration to our weary souls.

Continue to lean on Him, trusting in His unfailing love and grace. May you find peace in community, seeking support and understanding as you navigate your mental health journey. Remember, you are not alone, and there is always hope for brighter days ahead.

MINNINA M. SMITH

October

—

Overcoming Fear and Limiting Beliefs

October 1

Fearless Beginnings

Today's all about starting fresh, pushing past doubts, and diving into new beginnings with gusto. It's okay to feel those butterflies fluttering in your stomach; they're just a sign that you're on the brink of something incredible. Embrace the unknown, take that leap of faith, and trust in your ability to overcome any hurdles that come your way.

Remember, every journey starts with a single step, and you've got what it takes to make this one count. So go ahead, be bold, and let's kick off this adventure together with fearless determination and unwavering courage!

October 2

Breaking Boundaries

Today's about smashing those boundaries holding you back. It's about grabbing life by the reins, saying "I've got this," and diving headfirst into the unknown. Yeah, it's scary, but guess what?

You're stronger than you think. You've got a warrior spirit inside, ready to tackle whatever comes your way. So, take that leap, chase those dreams, and don't look back. Break those barriers with every step you take, knowing that with each one, you're one step closer to your best self. You've got this, and I'm cheering you on every step of the way!

October 3

Courageous Choices

Today, let's talk about taking courageous steps. It's about standing strong, even when fear tries to creep in. Remember, faith is like a sturdy rock beneath your feet, giving you the courage to move forward. Believe in yourself and in the power of divine guidance. Each choice you make, no matter how small, shapes your journey.

Embrace the unknown with a heart filled with faith, knowing that every step forward is a step toward growth. You're stronger than you realize, and with faith as your guide, you can conquer any challenge that comes your way. Keep choosing courage, my friend.

October 4

Conquering Doubt

Ever have those moments when you're like, "Can I really do this?" Doubts creeping in, making you question yourself? We've all been there! But guess what? You've got what it takes to conquer those doubts. Believe it! Look back at all the times you've faced challenges head-on and came out stronger. You're unstoppable!

So, when those doubts creep in again, remember your victories. You're capable, you're strong, and you've got a whole world of possibilities ahead. Keep pushing through, one step at a time. You've got this!

October 5

Brave Steps

Sometimes life throws us curveballs, right? But you know what? Every step you take, no matter how small, is a step of bravery. It's about facing those challenges head-on, with your chin up and your heart open.

Remember, you're not alone in this journey. There's a whole world of possibilities waiting for you, and each step you take brings you closer to your dreams. So be proud of those brave steps you're taking, and keep moving forward.

October 6

Facing Fears

It's just you and me for a moment. Let's talk about facing fears. We all have 'em, right? But guess what? You're not alone in this. There's a higher power watching over you, rooting for you every step of the way. So, when those fears start creeping in, take a deep breath and remember who's got your back.

You're stronger than you think, and you've got what it takes to push through. So go ahead, face those fears head-on, knowing that you're walking hand in hand with the One who gives you strength. You got this!

October 7

Bold Breakthroughs

You know those moments when you feel like you're stuck in a rut, but then suddenly, something shifts? That's a bold breakthrough! It's like breaking through a wall that's been holding you back. Maybe it's finally standing up to that nagging fear or taking a leap of faith into something new.

Whatever it is, embrace it! Bold breakthroughs are what propel us forward, pushing us beyond our limits and into new possibilities. So don't be afraid to embrace the changes and challenges that come your way. They could be the key to unlocking your next big adventure!

October 8

Resilient Resolve

Resilience, it's that inner strength we all have, you know? The power to bounce back when life throws us curveballs. It's not always easy, but it's what keeps us going. So, when things get tough, remember your resilient resolve. Take a deep breath, dust yourself off, and keep moving forward. You've got this! Trust in your ability to overcome whatever comes your way.

Let your resilience shine bright, showing the world what you're made of. Keep pushing through, and remember, tough times don't last, but tough people do.

October 9

Empowered Minds

You know what's awesome? Having a mind that's like a superhero cape, ready to conquer any challenge. Yup, that's you! Your mind is powerful, capable of amazing things. So rock this day with confidence and courage, knowing that you've got what it takes to handle whatever comes our way. Believe in yourself, trust your instincts, and keep shining bright.

Embrace the strength within you, and let it guide you towards your dreams. Unleash your empowered mind and show the world what we're made of. You've got this!

October 10

Strength Within

Deep within each of us lies a wellspring of strength waiting to be tapped into. It's that inner fire, that relentless spirit that keeps us going when the going gets tough. It's the courage to face our fears head-on, to push through the doubts and insecurities that hold us back.

Sometimes, we may not even realize the power we possess until we're faced with adversity. But trust me, it's there, deep within our souls, waiting to be unleashed. So, take a moment today to acknowledge the strength within you. You're stronger than you think, and you've got this today!

October 11

Defying Limits

Today, let's talk about defying limits. You know those moments when everyone says "you can't"? Well, forget that! You're capable of so much more than you think. Push those boundaries, challenge yourself, and show the world what you're made of.

Whether it's pursuing your dreams, overcoming obstacles, or just getting out of your comfort zone, remember that limits are meant to be broken. Embrace your inner rebel, embrace the unknown, and watch yourself soar. Life's too short to stay within the lines, so go ahead and defy those limits. You've got this!

October 12

Fearless Hearts

You have a courageous soul! Just a little reminder that you've got a heart of pure courage and strength. Even when fear tries to sneak up on you, remember that faith can help you push through anything.

It's okay to feel scared sometimes, but don't let it hold you back from all the amazing things waiting for you. Trust in your inner strength and the power above, and you'll see just how fearless you truly are. Keep shining your light, embracing the journey, and walking with faith every step of the way.

October 13

Courage Calls

Today, I want to chat about something important: courage. It's that spark inside you that says, "Hey, I can do this!" Life throws curveballs, but guess what? You've got what it takes to handle them. Trust me, even when it feels tough, know that you're not alone.

God is looking out for you, giving you that extra push when you need it most. So, take a deep breath, hold your head high, and step forward with courage. You've got this, and with faith guiding you, there's nothing you can't overcome. Keep shining bright!

October 14

Breaking Barriers

Barriers, you know, those walls we build around ourselves, whether it's fear, doubt, or insecurity. It's time to kick them down! You've got so much potential waiting to be unleashed. Take a deep breath, believe in yourself, and take that leap of faith.

Don't let anything hold you back. Life's too short to be confined by limitations. Embrace the challenges, embrace the unknown, and embrace your own strength. You've got this! Let's break those barriers together and step into a world of endless possibilities.

October 15

Conquering Challenges

Let's talk about kicking those challenges to the curb! Life's full of ups and downs, but you've got what it takes to conquer them all. Remember, every obstacle you face is just another opportunity to show how strong you are. Take a deep breath, put on your game face, and tackle those challenges head-on.

You've got resilience flowing through your veins, and nothing can hold you back. Keep pushing forward, and before you know it, you'll be standing tall on the other side, stronger and more victorious than ever. You've got this!

October 16

Boldly Forward

Today's all about taking those big, bold steps forward. Remember, God's got your back through it all. As Philippians 4:13 says, "I can do all things through Christ who strengthens me."

So, let's push past those doubts and fears, knowing that we're capable of more than we think. Embrace that inner strength, and let's tackle whatever comes our way head-on.

October 17

Overcoming Obstacles

Have you ever felt stuck? We've all been there. Life throws curveballs, but guess what? You're stronger than you think. Remember Philippians 4:13: "I can do all things through Christ who strengthens me." So, take a deep breath, put on your armor of faith, and face those obstacles head-on.

Believe in yourself because God believes in you. You've got this! Keep pushing forward, and before you know it, you'll be on the other side, stronger and wiser than ever. Just keep going, and remember, every obstacle is just a steppingstone on the path to greatness.

October 18

Courage Over Fear

When we face challenges, it's easy to let fear take the wheel. But guess what? You're tougher than fear. Yeah, that's right! It's like looking fear in the eye and saying, "Not today!" You've got this, seriously.

It's about pushing past those doubts, taking that leap, and embracing the unknown with open arms. Life's an adventure, right? So, don't let fear hold you back from experiencing every bit of it. Courage isn't the absence of fear; it's walking alongside it, hand in hand, and saying, "I'm moving forward anyway." You've got courage running through your veins. Let it shine!

October 19

Rising Above

When life hits hard, remember this: you're made of tough stuff. We all stumble, we all fall, but guess what? We rise, every single time. It's not about avoiding the storm, it's about dancing in the rain, letting the thunder fuel your fire. So, when you're feeling down and out, remember your strength. You've conquered mountains before, and you'll conquer them again. Embrace your scars, wear them like badges of honor.

They're proof of battles fought and won. So, chin up, my friend. You're not just surviving; you're thriving, rising above it all, stronger than ever before.

October 20

Fearless Living

Ever felt like fear's holding you back? I have been there too. But you know what? We're tougher than we realize. Let's push fear aside and live boldly. It's about confronting our fears, taking those first steps, and welcoming life's challenges.

Sure, it won't be a walk in the park, but remember: God hasn't given us a spirit of fear, but of power, love, and a sound mind (2 Timothy 1:7). So let's tackle this journey together – fearlessly pursuing our dreams and savoring every moment. Believe me, it's worth it. We're in this together, and we're stronger than fear!

October 21

Limitless Potential

There is nothing you can't do, seriously! Look at all those dreams dancing around in your head. They're there for a reason, waiting for you to chase after them. You've got skills, talents, and an unstoppable spirit.

Don't let anyone tell you otherwise. Sure, there might be hurdles, but you've already hurdled plenty, right? Keep that momentum going. You're like a shooting star, blazing through the night sky, lighting up the world with your brilliance. So, what's next? The sky's the limit, my friend, and even that's debatable. So, go ahead, show the world what you're made of!

October 22

Courageous Journeys

It's okay if you're the first one in your family to do what you're doing. You have no other roadmap but the Lord Himself guiding you. It might feel lonely at times, but remember, pioneers always lead the way. Your courage to step into the unknown paves the path for others to follow.

Embrace your journey with confidence and faith. You're creating a legacy of bravery and resilience. Trust in the wisdom of your heart and the guidance of God. Your journey may be unique, but you're never alone. Keep walking, knowing that each step forward is a testament to your courage and strength.

October 23

Beyond Fear

Your life is so much more than your current moment. Imagine all that it could be if you just did that thing, started that project, or worked towards the you that you've always seen yourself being. It's time to stop being scared, friend, and just do it.

Beyond fear lies a world of possibilities waiting for you. Embrace the uncertainty, step out of your comfort zone, and watch as your dreams unfold before your eyes. You have the strength and courage within you to overcome any obstacle. Believe in yourself, take that leap of faith, and let your true potential shine.

October 24

Breaking Free

Today, let's talk about "Breaking Free." You know, like breaking out of old habits, old patterns, old ways of thinking that hold us back. It's like shedding an old skin, stepping into something new and exciting.

It's not always easy. Nah, it can be downright scary sometimes. But hey, the view from the other side? It's worth it. So let's take a step, maybe a leap, towards something better today. Let's break free from what's been holding us back and step boldly into the life we want to live. You got this.

October 25

Bold Beliefs

In life, we gotta hold on tight to what we believe in, you know? Like that verse says, "For God gave us a spirit not of fear but of power and love and self-control." So, let's walk tall with faith, even when doubts creep in. We're stronger than we think, stronger than fear itself.

Remember, faith ain't just wishful thinking; it's trustin' in somethin' bigger, somethin' divine. So, let's hold our heads high, stand firm in our beliefs, and tackle each day with boldness. With God by our side, there's nothin' we can't face.

October 26

Empowered Choices

Hey there! Today's all about calling the shots and owning your decisions. It's about recognizing that every choice you make has power, whether big or small.
So, embrace your freedom to choose and trust yourself to make the best decisions for your journey. Remember, you've got this! It's all about taking those steps, no matter how small they may seem, towards the life you envision for yourself.
So, go ahead, make those empowered choices, and watch as they lead you closer to your dreams. You've got the power within you, so go ahead and own it!

October 27

Fearless Futures

Today's all about taking that leap, shaking off those doubts, and embracing the awesome potential within you. It's time to blow the roof off your future! You've got this, seriously. Sure, there might be some bumps along the way, but trust me, you're stronger than you think. Believe in yourself, chase those dreams, and don't let fear hold you back.

Your future is waiting, and it's ready for some serious greatness. So, let's kick those limiting beliefs to the curb and step boldly into those fearless futures. You're unstoppable, my friend. Let's do this!

October 28

Stepping Out Strong

It's time to step out strong and embrace what lies ahead. Life's full of twists and turns, but you've got what it takes to navigate through them. Remember, it's okay to stumble along the way – it's all part of the journey.

Just keep pushing forward with courage and determination. You've got a fire within you that's ready to blaze brighter than ever before. So, take those bold steps, face your fears, and show the world what you're made of. Your strength is unmatched, and your resilience knows no bounds. Keep shining, keep striving, and keep stepping out strong.

October 29

Dare to Dream

Hey there, it's time to take that leap of faith and chase after your dreams. Sure, it might seem daunting, but trust me, you've got what it takes. Remember, every big achievement starts with a dream, so why not make yours a reality? Embrace the journey, setbacks and all, and keep pushing forward.

You never know what incredible things lie ahead until you dare to dream and go after them. So, let's roll up our sleeves, get out there, and make those dreams happen. You've got this!

October 30

Be Unstoppable

It's time to unleash your inner powerhouse and be unstoppable. Remember, setbacks are just setups for comebacks. You've got the strength, the grit, and the determination to tackle anything that comes your way. Don't let doubts or fears hold you back.

Embrace challenges as opportunities to grow and learn. Keep pushing forward with courage and resilience. You're capable of achieving incredible things when you believe in yourself. So, take that leap, chase those dreams, and show the world what you're made of. You've got this!

October 31

Empowered Beginnings

You know what's awesome about waking up each day? It's like hitting the reset button on life. Another chance to get it right, to do better, to be better. As we wrap up this month and gear up for the next, keep in mind all the possibilities that lie ahead.

It's like a fresh canvas waiting for your masterpiece. So, seize the day, embrace the challenges, and welcome the opportunities with open arms. Your journey is just beginning, and with each new dawn, you have the chance to create something truly amazing. So go on, step into those empowered beginnings!

MINNINA M. SMITH

November

—

Building Healthy Relationships

November 1

Nurturing Boundaries

Ah, here we go again with the word "boundaries"! Lol, but seriously, they're like the guardrails on a highway – essential for a smooth ride. Setting boundaries isn't about being mean; it's about respecting yourself and others. It's saying, "Hey, this is where I draw the line." And you know what? That's okay!

It's about knowing your limits and honoring them. So, let's embrace our boundaries like a cozy blanket on a chilly night – comforting and necessary for our well-being. Remember, it's not about keeping people out; it's about inviting the right ones in.

November 2

Healing from Heartbreak

It's tough when love hits a rough patch. But trust me, you're tougher. It's okay to feel broken right now. Let those tears flow, let that pain out. But remember, this heartbreak won't define you forever. You're on a journey of healing, and each day, you're taking small steps forward.

Surround yourself with people who lift you up, do things that make you smile, and most importantly, be kind to yourself. In time, the hurt will ease, and you'll find a new sense of strength and resilience within you. You're not alone in this, and brighter days are ahead.

November 3

Cultivating Compassion

Compassion is a deep awareness of and sympathy for another's suffering, accompanied by a desire to alleviate that suffering. It involves feeling empathy towards others, understanding their challenges, and being motivated to help them in whatever way possible. Compassion often goes beyond just feeling sorry for someone; it involves taking action to support and care for those in need. It's all about showing kindness and understanding to others, even when they're going through tough times.

You know, sometimes life can throw some curveballs, and it's easy to get caught up in our own struggles. But taking a moment to see things from someone else's perspective can make all the difference. So, whether it's lending a listening ear to a friend or simply offering a smile to a stranger, let's make compassion a part of our everyday lives. You never know how much it might brighten someone's day!

November 4

Overcoming Loneliness

Loneliness isn't just about being physically alone. It's that ache deep down when you feel disconnected, like no one gets you. But here's the thing, you're not alone in feeling this way. It's a common human experience, and it's okay to feel it sometimes.

Just remember, even when it feels like everyone else has turned their back on you, there's someone who never will. In Hebrews 13:5, God says, "I will never leave you nor forsake you." It's like a warm hug from the Almighty, a reminder that you're never truly alone. So, when loneliness creeps in, lean into that promise and find solace in the presence of the One who sticks closer than a brother.

November 5

Embracing Vulnerability

Can we talk about something real—vulnerability. It's scary, right? Putting yourself out there, exposing your flaws, fears, and uncertainties. But you know what? It's also where the wonders unfold. When you let down your guard, you invite connection and authenticity into your life. Sure, it might feel uncomfortable at first, but trust me, it's worth it.

Whether you're starting a new relationship or deepening an existing one, embracing vulnerability is key. It's about being raw, honest, and unapologetically yourself. So, let's take a leap together, shall we? Embrace the messiness, the imperfections, and the unknowns. Because that's where love and growth thrive.

November 6

Reconnecting with Loved Ones

November rolls around, and suddenly, we're drawn to reconnect with our tribe. But let's face it, the holiday vibe hits differently for each of us. Some feel the warmth, while others, not so much. Regardless, it's a time for reaching out, sharing laughs, and maybe even mending fences.

We'll gather, not just for turkey, but for tales and toasts. Amidst the chaos, let's remember the quiet ones, the ones struggling to find their place in the festive buzz. Let's extend a hand, an ear, and a heart, for it's in these small acts that we truly reconnect and find the essence of the season.

November 7

Forgiving Yourself

Here's a little wisdom for today. Look, we all mess up sometimes, it's part of being human. But here's the thing: holding onto guilt and shame doesn't do anyone any good, especially not you.

So why not cut yourself some slack? Give yourself the same grace you'd give to a friend who made a mistake. Learn from it, grow, and move forward. You deserve to be happy and at peace with yourself. So, take a deep breath, let go of that burden, and step into the light. You've got this.

November 8

Setting Healthy Expectations

Let's chat about setting some healthy expectations today. You know, it's all about finding that sweet spot where you're not putting too much pressure on yourself or others. It's like giving yourself permission to be human, to make mistakes, and to learn and grow from them.

Expectations can be tricky sometimes, but when you set them with kindness and understanding, it can make all the difference. So, let's take a moment to check in with ourselves and see if our expectations are serving us well. Remember, it's okay to adjust them as needed to keep things balanced and positive!

November 9

Communicating Effectively

How we communicate is a big deal. You see, how we talk to others says a lot about us. It's not just the words we say, but how we say 'em, ya know? Are we really listening? Are we being clear and respectful?

Sometimes it's easy to get caught up in our own thoughts, but effective communication is all about connecting with others, understanding them, and making sure we're understood too. So, let's strive to communicate in a way that brings us closer together, 'cause good communication? That's the key to great relationships.

November 10

Strengthening Support Systems

In life, we're blessed with some real gems, you know? Those friends and family who always got your back, no matter what. They're like a warm hug on a cold day, or that first sip of coffee in the morning—pure comfort.

We lean on each other, laugh with each other, and lift each other up when times get tough. And you know what? It's not just luck. It's a little sprinkle of grace, a dash of faith, and a whole lot of love that holds us together. So let's keep strengthening those support systems and keep the good vibes flowing.

November 11

Managing Family Dynamics

Navigating family dynamics can be like a wild roller coaster ride, full of twists and turns. We all have those moments when we feel like throwing our hands up in frustration! But amidst the chaos, there's also a lot of love and laughter. Remember, it's okay to set boundaries and take time for yourself when things get overwhelming. Don't be afraid to speak your truth and express your needs.

Sometimes, a little humor goes a long way in diffusing tension. Embrace the quirks and imperfections that make your family unique, and cherish the moments of connection and understanding.

November 12

Building Trust in Relationships

In every relationship, trust is the glue that holds everything together. It's not always easy to build, but it's worth it. Start by being honest and transparent, and show that you're reliable. Listen actively and empathize with others' feelings. Be patient, trust takes time.

Remember, trust isn't just given; it's earned through consistent actions and genuine intentions. Sometimes, it means taking a leap of faith, believing in the goodness of others despite past hurts. So, take small steps, cherish the moments of vulnerability, and watch as the bonds of trust grow stronger, enriching your relationships in ways you never imagined.

November 13

Finding Balance in Relationships

Navigating the hustle without losing heart? Totally doable. So, how do we juggle climbing the career ladder while keeping our relationships intact? It's about finding the sweet spot. Like, maybe scheduling date nights or unplugging during meals, carve out time for family dinners, or just chill sessions. It's about quality over quantity, ya know?

Don't sweat the small stuff; instead, focus on what truly matters. Communication is key. Open up about your goals and fears. And remember, it's okay to ask for support. Finding balance ain't about perfection; it's about making intentional choices that align with your values and bring you closer to those you love.

November 14

Cultivating Empathy

In life's dance, understanding the rhythm of others' hearts brings harmony. It's like tuning into different radio frequencies, catching their vibe. Maybe it's a hug or a listening ear, but often it's simply acknowledging their story. We all carry invisible burdens, scars unseen by the naked eye.

When we step into someone else's shoes, we understand their journey a little better. Empathy, it's like planting seeds of kindness, watering them with love. It's a daily practice, one that softens hearts and fosters connections. So, let's walk this path together, cultivating empathy in every step we take.

November 15

Handling Relationship Conflicts

Ooh, this is a good one today. Let's talk about handling relationship conflicts. We all have those moments when tensions run high and disagreements arise. It's easy to let emotions take over, but here's the thing: conflicts can actually be opportunities for growth.

Take a deep breath and approach the situation with empathy and understanding. Listen actively, express yourself calmly, and be open to finding common ground. Remember, it's okay to disagree as long as we do it respectfully. By navigating conflicts with care and compassion, we can strengthen our relationships and foster deeper connections with those we love.

November 16

Building Self-Esteem

How I feel about myself is what truly matters. You see, self-esteem isn't about impressing others or meeting society's standards. It's about loving and accepting yourself just the way you are. So, embrace your quirks, celebrate your victories, and forgive your flaws. You're worthy of love, success, and happiness, simply because you exist.

Remember, self-esteem grows from within, not from external validation. So, be kind to yourself, nourish your soul, and believe in your worth. You're a masterpiece in progress, flawed yet beautiful, and deserving of all the love and respect in the world. Shine on, dear soul.

November 17

Letting Go of Resentment

Sometimes, it's like carrying bricks in your heart, isn't it? That weight of resentment can really drag you down. But hey, it's time to let go. Trust me, I get it. It's not easy, but holding onto that bitterness only hurts you in the end.

So take a deep breath, release that tension, and let it all go. Remember, forgiveness isn't about saying what they did was okay; it's about freeing yourself from the chains of anger and bitterness. So, go ahead, let go of that resentment, and watch how much lighter your heart feels. You deserve that peace.

November 18

Practicing Active Listening

Ever feel like you're talking to a wall? Like you could earn a dollar for every time you've had to ask, "Are you even listening?" We've all been there. But what if I told you that active listening isn't just about hearing words—it's about understanding feelings, too?

It's about being fully present, tuning in not just with your ears but with your heart. So, let's flip the script. Today, let's practice active listening. Let's give each other the gift of being truly heard, understood, and valued. Because sometimes, the best thing we can do is to simply listen with love.

November 19

Embracing Imperfection

Hey there, just a little reminder: nobody's perfect, and that's okay! Life's all about embracing our quirks and imperfections. So, let's celebrate our unique selves and all the beautiful messiness that comes with it. It's in those little flaws where our true beauty lies, you know?

So go ahead, let your imperfections shine bright like the stars in the night sky. Remember, you're perfectly imperfect, and that's what makes you so wonderfully you. So keep on rocking your authenticity and embracing every part of who you are. You're amazing just the way you are!

November 20

Prioritizing Self-Care

Don't forget to put yourself first sometimes. Self-care isn't just bubble baths and face masks; it's about nurturing your mind, body, and spirit. Take a break, go for a walk, or indulge in your favorite hobby.

Listen to your needs and honor them without guilt. It's okay to say no to things that drain you and yes to things that nourish your soul. Remember, you can't pour from an empty cup. So, give yourself permission to rest, recharge, and show yourself some love. You deserve it, always.

November 21

Releasing Toxic Relationships

This is a major one. Sometimes, you gotta let go of the toxic stuff in your life to make room for the good vibes. It's like cleaning out your closet, you know? Sure, it might be tough at first, but once you declutter, you'll feel so much lighter.

Trust me, you deserve relationships that lift you up, not drag you down. So, take a deep breath, gather your courage, and start setting those boundaries. You got this. And remember, it's not about cutting people off, it's about choosing yourself and creating space for positivity to flow.

November 22

Expressing Gratitude in Relationships

We often forget how powerful a simple "thank you" can be. Let's sprinkle gratitude everywhere in our relationships, from the big things to the small gestures.

Maybe it's appreciating your partner's efforts or acknowledging a friend's support. Gratitude fuels connections and deepens bonds. It's like watering a plant; it helps love and friendship grow. So, next time someone does something kind, let them know how much it means to you. It's not just about saying the words; it's about genuinely feeling thankful and expressing it. Gratitude turns ordinary moments into cherished memories.

November 23

Embracing Change Together

In any relationship with those you love, change will be necessary. It's the natural ebb and flow of life, isn't it? We grow, we evolve, and sometimes that means our relationships do too. It's not always easy, I know. But together, we can navigate these changes with grace and understanding.

Let's lean on each other, communicate openly, and embrace the journey together. Change doesn't have to be scary; it can be an opportunity for growth and deeper connection. So let's take each other's hands and walk boldly into the unknown, trusting that our love will guide us through.

November 24

Respecting Differences

In this journey of life, we're all different, like a patchwork quilt woven with diverse threads. It's in these differences that we find our strength, our beauty, and our uniqueness. Let's celebrate our diversity, embracing the colors, the textures, and the patterns that make each of us special.

Let's learn from one another, listen to each other's stories, and respect each other's perspectives. For it's in this tapestry of differences that we find unity, understanding, and love. So let's honor and respect the beautiful diversity that surrounds us, knowing that it's what makes our world so vibrant and alive.

November 25

Fostering Healthy Communication

Today let's chat about keeping those lines open, not just with others, but with yourself too. It's all about being real, sharing your thoughts, and really listening to others. Sometimes it's hard, but it's worth it. It's about understanding, not just hearing. So, let's promise to speak from the heart, without judgment or fear.

Let's create a space where everyone feels safe to express themselves, knowing they'll be heard. Because when we communicate openly and honestly, we build trust and deepen our connections. So, here's to fostering healthy communication – let's keep those conversations flowing and hearts growing.

November 26

Honoring Personal Boundaries

Continue to set those boundaries – not just physical ones, but the ones that guard our hearts and minds. It's like carving out a safe space for yourself in this wild world. You deserve that, you know? Don't let anyone make you feel guilty for looking out for yourself.

Remember it's not selfish; it's self-love. When you respect your boundaries, others learn to do the same. So, take a step back when you need to, say no without hesitation, and protect your peace fiercely. Your well-being is non-negotiable, and anyone who truly cares about you will understand that.

November 27

Building Mutual Respect

In life's intricate dance, mutual respect forms the foundation of genuine connection. It's about honoring each other's uniqueness, recognizing our shared humanity. When we listen with open hearts and minds, acknowledging perspectives, we foster understanding and harmony.

It's the small gestures of kindness, the genuine smiles exchanged, that build bridges between souls. Let's embrace empathy, appreciating the beauty in our diversity. In disagreements, let's seek resolution with compassion and grace. Together, let's create a space where everyone feels valued and heard. In this journey of mutual respect, we sow seeds of love and unity, enriching our lives and those around us.

MINNINA M. SMITH

November 28

Fostering Healthy Workplace Communication

Though most may be off from work and on holiday during this time of the year, a majority are not so, this mindful practice may be helpful. Navigating workplace communication can feel like sailing uncharted waters. Yet, amidst the sometimes what may seem rigmarole, emails and meetings, or procedural task there's a chance for genuine connection. Start by actively listening to your colleagues' ideas and concerns, fostering an environment where everyone feels heard.

Remember, it's okay to express your thoughts respectfully too. Embrace constructive feedback as a tool for growth rather than criticism. Approach conversations with empathy, understanding that each person brings their unique perspective to the table. By fostering healthy communication at work, you're not just enhancing productivity but also building stronger, more meaningful relationships that uplift everyone involved. Let's sail these seas together, stars.

November 29

Respect Yourself

Just wanted to drop a little reminder your way: you are worthy of respect. Yup, that's right! It starts from within, you know? Treat yourself like the superstar you are. Set those boundaries, stand tall, and don't settle for anything less than you deserve. When you respect yourself, you're showing the world your true worth.

So, go ahead, embrace your uniqueness, honor your feelings, and never forget to give yourself a pat on the back. You've got this! Keep shining bright, superstar!

November 30

Nurturing Emotional Intimacy

At the end of this month, let's take a moment to appreciate the beauty of emotional intimacy. It's about connecting on a deeper level, sharing our fears, hopes, and dreams without hesitation. It's those late-night conversations where words flow freely and hearts intertwine. It's the laughter shared over inside jokes and the comfort found in silent understanding.

Let's nurture this precious bond, cherishing every moment we get to spend with those who truly see us for who we are. Together, let's create a space where vulnerability is welcomed, and love flows abundantly. Here's to nurturing emotional intimacy every step of the way

December

—

Reflection And Renewal During The Last Month Of The Year

December 1

Coping with Seasonal Stress

Feeling the weight of holiday? Take a breath, you're not alone. It's easy to get swept up in the chaos, but remember, it's okay to slow down. Find your cozy spot, wrap yourself in a warm blanket, and sip on that favorite hot drink.

Embrace the little moments of joy: a crackling fireplace, twinkling lights, or a hug from a loved one. Allow yourself to let go of perfection and simply be present. You've got this! Remember, it's not about the grand gestures, but the quiet, soul-nourishing moments that truly matter during this season.

December 2

Embracing The Holiday Season

Hey there, it's that time of the year again, and I know it can be tough. The holidays, right? They're supposed to be all about joy and cheer, but sometimes they just make us feel all sorts of things. Maybe it's because of memories we'd rather forget, or people we wish were still here with us.

But you know what? Even in the midst of all that, there's still light. Remember the reason for the season, that little spark of hope that never fades away? Hold onto that, and let it guide you through. You're not alone in this journey.

December 3

Finding Peace Amid Chaos

In December, life can feel like a whirlwind, but amidst the chaos, peace is waiting to be found. Take a moment to step back, breathe, and let go of the hustle. It's okay to slow down, to embrace the quiet moments, to find solace in the stillness.

Whether it's sitting by a crackling fire, sipping hot cocoa, or taking a quiet walk in nature, allow yourself to be present. In these simple moments, you'll discover a sense of calm that soothes your soul and reminds you that peace is always within reach, even in the busiest of times.

December 4

Navigating Family Dynamics

As we get further into December, let's talk about family – the good, the bad, and the sometimes non-existent. Whether you're gearing up for fun-filled gatherings or bracing yourself for challenging dynamics, this month can stir up a mix of emotions. It's okay if your family time isn't picture-perfect like in the movies.

Remember, everyone's journey is different. Embrace the chaos, cherish the laughter, and hold onto those moments of connection, no matter how fleeting they may seem. Together, let's navigate the twists and turns of family life with grace, understanding, and maybe a little bit of humor thrown in.

December 5

Cultivating Gratitude Daily

It's a good time to be thankful, you know? Like, even when things get tough, finding something to appreciate can lift your spirits. Maybe it's the little things, like a warm cup of coffee in the morning or a hug from a loved one.

Or maybe it's the big stuff, like having a roof over your head or good health. Gratitude isn't just about saying thanks; it's about feeling it deep down, you know? So let's make it a habit to find something to be grateful for every day. It might just change your whole perspective on life.

December 6

Overcoming Loneliness Together

For some this season, some experience extreme loneliness to the point of depression. But we're not alone in feeling lonely. It's tough, but reaching out to others, even in small ways, can make a big difference. A phone call, a text, or a chat over coffee can brighten someone's day, including yours.

And remember, it's okay to ask for help if you're struggling. We're all in this together, navigating the ups and downs of life. So let's lift each other up, offer a listening ear, and spread a little kindness. Together, we can overcome loneliness and find connection.

December 7

Finding Joy in Small Moments

Life's about cherishing those little things, ya know? Like sipping coffee on a chilly morning, or sharing a laugh with a friend. It's in those simple moments that joy sneaks in, reminding us of life's beauty.

So next time you're feeling down, take a sec to notice the small stuff – the sun peeking through the clouds, the smell of fresh rain, the warmth of a cozy blanket. Embrace these moments, soak 'em in. 'Cause in the end, it's these little joys that make life truly special, filling our hearts with warmth and gratitude.

December 8

Managing Holiday Expectations

The holidays can get real crazy, right? We all have these big ideas about how perfect everything should be. But let's be real - life ain't perfect, and neither are the holidays. It's okay to let go of those picture-perfect expectations and just enjoy the moment, however messy it may be.

Sometimes the best memories come from the unplanned, imperfect moments. So this holiday season, cut yourself some slack, and let things unfold naturally. Embrace the chaos, laugh at the mishaps, and cherish the little moments of joy. After all, those imperfect moments are what make the holidays memorable.

MINNINA M. SMITH

December 9

Surviving Seasonal Blues

    Are feeling those seasonal blues? You're not alone. Winter can bring a whole lot of emotions, but hang in there. Remember, it's okay to feel down sometimes. Take it easy on yourself, indulge in some self-care—maybe a cozy night in with your favorite movie or a warm cup of tea.

    Reach out to loved ones for support, or maybe just give yourself a little extra TLC. And hey, spring's just around the corner, bringing with it new beginnings and brighter days. You've got this. Just take it one day at a time, and don't forget to breathe.

December 10

Dealing with Financial Strain

Money can be a real headache sometimes, right? Bills piling up, unexpected expenses popping out of nowhere—it's like a never-ending cycle. But hey, you're not alone in this. We've all been there. It's tough, but remember, tough times don't last forever.

Take a deep breath, prioritize what needs to be paid first, and maybe brainstorm some creative ways to make a little extra cash. And hey, don't forget to reach out if you need a shoulder to lean on. We're all in this together, and together, we'll get through it. You got this!

MINNINA M. SMITH

December 11

Seeking Solitude for Self-Care

Taking some alone time ain't selfish, it's necessary for your well-being. We all need a breather from the noise sometimes. So, find your cozy spot, brew your favorite cuppa, and just be with yourself. Use this time to recharge, reflect, and rejuvenate.

Maybe it's a walk in the park or a quiet evening with a good book. Whatever it is, make it yours. Treat yourself with kindness and compassion. Remember, self-care ain't a luxury; it's a necessity. So, take that step, carve out that me-time, and watch how it transforms your soul. You deserve it, always.

December 12

Forgiving Past Hurts

Hey there, it's time to let go of that baggage weighing you down. Holding onto past hurts only drains your energy and blocks your blessings. Forgiveness isn't about saying what happened was okay; it's about freeing yourself from the grip of resentment.

Trust me, it's like lifting a weight off your shoulders. Take a deep breath, release the negativity, and open your heart to healing. Remember, forgiveness is a gift you give yourself. So, take that step forward, embrace the peace that comes with letting go, and make room for brighter days ahead. You've got this!

December 13

Letting Go of Perfectionism

It may not be perfect this year, but guess what? That's okay. Life's not about being flawless; it's about being real. So what if things don't go as planned? Embrace the messiness, the imperfections. They're what make life interesting.

Give yourself permission to let go of that pressure to be perfect. Take a deep breath, exhale the stress, and just be. Embrace the beautiful chaos of life. Remember, it's not about having it all together; it's about being present in the moment. So let's ditch perfectionism and celebrate the wonderfully imperfect journey we're on.

December 14

Setting Healthy Boundaries

You know, sometimes we gotta set those boundaries, you know what I mean? It's not about shutting people out or being mean, it's about taking care of ourselves. It's like saying, "Hey, this is my space, and I need to protect it." It's okay to say no sometimes, to protect your peace and sanity.

Setting boundaries is like drawing a line in the sand, saying, "This is where I stand, and I won't let anyone cross it." It's about showing respect for yourself and teaching others how to respect you too. So, don't be afraid to set those healthy boundaries and stand your ground.

December 15

Honoring Loved Ones Lost

Having lost my fair share of loved ones, especially my parents, I get how tough this process can be. Grieving ain't easy, and it's okay to feel all sorts of ways about it. Some days, it feels like a heavy weight on your chest, and other days, it's just a dull ache in the background. But remember, it's okay to take your time with it.

There's no rush, no deadline to meet. Let yourself feel whatever you need to feel, and know that you're not alone in this journey. We'll get through it together, one step at a time.

December 16

Spreading Love and Kindness

Can we spread love and kindness today? It's about doing small things that can make a big difference. Maybe it's a smile to a stranger, holding the door open, or simply saying thank you.

These little acts of kindness ripple out into the world, touching hearts and brightening days. And guess what? When you spread love, you receive it back in return. It's like magic! So, let's make spreading love and kindness a daily habit. Together, we can create a world that's a little brighter and a lot more beautiful. Let's start today!

December 17

Finding Hope in Darkness

In those tough times when it feels like you're stumbling around in the dark, hold tight to hope. It's that tiny spark that flickers even when everything seems dim. Remember, even the darkest nights lead to brighter days.

Trust that better times are just around the corner. Believe that you're stronger than you think and capable of overcoming any obstacle. Surround yourself with love and positivity, and let that guide you through the shadows. So, when life feels gloomy, keep your chin up and your heart open. There's always a glimmer of hope waiting to light up your path.

December 18

Embracing Imperfections

Remember it's okay to be imperfect. We all have our quirks and flaws, and that's what makes us unique. Embrace those imperfections; they're what make you real. Don't let society's standards dictate your worth. Instead, celebrate your authenticity and embrace who you are, flaws and all.

Remember, perfection is overrated. It's the imperfections that add character to our lives and make us relatable. So, be kind to yourself, accept your flaws, and know that you're perfectly imperfect, just the way you're meant to be. Let's navigate this journey together, embracing every aspect of ourselves along the way.

December 19

Seeking Support in Community

When life gets tough, we don't have to go at it alone. Sometimes, all we need is a little help from our friends and neighbors. Whether it's a listening ear, a shoulder to lean on, or just a friendly face to brighten our day, reaching out to our community can make all the difference. Together, we can navigate life's challenges and celebrate its joys.

So don't hesitate to lean on those around you when you need a hand and be there to offer your support in return. In our community, we're all in this together.

December 20

Coping with Grief During Holidays

Facing the holidays after losing someone dear can feel like trekking uphill in heavy snow, it's freezing cold and you're by yourself. Memories flood in, both sweet and sorrowful. It's okay to feel a mix of emotions – anger, sadness, even numbness. Give yourself grace; there's no playbook for this.

Surround yourself with supportive folks who understand your journey. Maybe start a new tradition to honor your loved one's memory. Light a candle, share stories, or visit their favorite spot. And remember, it's okay to step back if it's all too much. Take it one moment at a time and know you're not alone in this.

December 21

Celebrating Simple Joys

Ah, can you feel it? The cozy vibes of the season are just spreading joy everywhere! For me, it's all about those hot cocoa moments, you know? Wrapping up in a warm blanket, sipping slowly, and just soaking in the goodness.

What about you? What brings that sparkle to your eyes during this special time? Maybe it's the twinkling lights, the laughter of loved ones, or simply taking a moment to appreciate the beauty around us. Let's cherish these simple joys together and make every moment count!

December 22

Managing Holiday Expectations

The holidays can be chaotic sometimes, lol. We're bombarded with images of perfect celebrations and happy families. But reality? It's often not picture-perfect. Maybe Aunt Sue's green bean casserole is a flop, or you can't afford those fancy gifts. It's okay. Take a breath. Remember, it's about being together, not perfect decorations or expensive presents. Lower those expectations a bit.

Focus on what truly matters: love, laughter, and connection. Embrace the chaos, laugh at the mishaps, and cherish the moments with loved ones. That's what makes the holidays truly special. So, relax, and enjoy the imperfect magic of the season.

December 23

Reconnecting with Faith

Faith is such a vital part of life, y'know? It's like having this anchor that keeps you grounded when life gets wild. Sometimes, you gotta take a step back, breathe, and remember what you believe in.

That faith? It's like a flicker of light in the darkness, guiding you through tough times. It's about trusting that there's something bigger out there, something watching over you, nudging you forward. So, take a moment today to reconnect with that faith of yours. Let it fill you up with hope, strength, and a whole lotta love. You got this.

December 24

Letting Light into the Darkness

When life feels heavy and the shadows seem to loom large, it's hard to see the light. But remember, even in the darkest of nights, there's a glimmer of hope waiting to be found. Sometimes, it's the little things—a kind word, a warm embrace, a moment of peace—that can brighten our path.

So, let's open our hearts to the possibility of joy, even amidst the darkness. Let's choose to focus on the sparks of light that shine through, guiding us forward with warmth and reassurance. Together, we'll illuminate the darkness and find our way to brighter days ahead.

December 25

The Reason For The Season

Let me introduce you to a man. He's not just any man, he's the ultimate game-changer, the one who turns lives around and hearts upside down. He's the one who walked on water, fed thousands with a few loaves and fishes, and healed the sick with just a touch.

He's the man who showed us love like no other, who forgave even when he was betrayed, and who sacrificed everything for us. He's the light in our darkest moments, the hope in our despair, and the joy in our sorrow.

He's the reason we celebrate, the reason we believe, and the reason we have eternal life. His name is Jesus Christ. You should get to know him if you don't know him yet. Trust me, he's worth it.

December 26

Reflecting on the Year's Lessons

As we wind down the year, it's time to look back and see what we've learned. Maybe we stumbled a bit, but each misstep brought a lesson. Life's like that, isn't it?

Sometimes we need to trip to find our footing. So, let's take a moment to think about what this year taught us. Maybe it's patience or resilience. Perhaps it's the power of love or the strength of community. Whatever it is, let's hold onto those lessons tight. They're the gems we carry into the new year, guiding us through the ups and downs ahead.

December 27

Cultivating Inner Peace

Reminder when you feel like life is a whirlwind. I get it. We all need a slice of peace in the chaos sometimes. Take a breather, close your eyes, and let your worries melt away.

Find that quiet corner, whether it's a cozy nook at home or a peaceful spot in nature. Breathe in, breathe out. Let your mind wander to the good stuff. Think of that moment that made you laugh until your belly hurt. Hold onto that feeling. Let it fill you up. That's your inner peace right there. Nurture it. Cherish it. You got this.

December 28

Holding onto Hope

When everything's tough, and you're feeling like you're stuck in a storm with no end in sight, just hang on. Yeah, life can throw some crazy curveballs, and sometimes it feels like the hits just keep on coming. But here's the thing - even in the darkest moments, there's a glimmer of hope.

It might be small, barely a flicker, but it's there. Hold onto it like your life depends on it, because in a way, it does. Hope keeps us going, keeps us pushing forward, even when it feels like we're barely treading water. So, when life gets tough, don't give up. Hold onto hope with everything you've got.

December 29

Finding Strength in Vulnerability

Can we say the word vulnerability today. You know, that feeling of being exposed, raw, and maybe even a bit scared. But guess what? It's okay to feel that way sometimes. In fact, it takes guts to embrace vulnerability.

It means letting down our guard and showing our true selves, flaws and all. And you know what's cool? When we're vulnerable, we're actually pretty darn strong. It takes courage to open up, to share our struggles, fears, and insecurities. But in doing so, we invite connection, empathy, and understanding into our lives. So, don't be afraid to let your guard down. Embrace your vulnerability, because that's where your true strength lies.

December 30

Rekindling Relationships

Now, this can be done with those long-lost friendships or romantic relationships. Before you rekindle, be sure it's something worth your time. Your energy is too precious to waste on anything less than genuine connections.

Take a moment to reflect on what you truly desire from these relationships. Is there mutual respect and understanding? Are there shared values and goals? If so, take the step to reconnect. If not, it's okay to let go and focus on nurturing relationships that uplift and support you. Trust your instincts and prioritize your emotional well-being.

December 31

Embracing Self-Care Practices

It's crucial to take care of yourself, you know? Sometimes life gets crazy, but don't forget about you. Whether it's a bubble bath, a walk in the park, or just chilling with a good book, find what makes you feel good and do it.

You deserve it! Self-care isn't selfish; it's necessary for your well-being. So, take a breather, recharge those batteries, and remember as you head into all that the next year will bring, know that you matter. You're worth investing time and energy into, so go ahead and pamper yourself a little. You'll feel so much better for it, trust me. Wishing you a blessed and prosperous new year ahead, each and every year!

If you enjoyed this book or would like to inquire about coaching services offered by Minnina M. Smith please head over to the website below:

www.thatdoseofencouragement.com

About The Author

Minnina M. Smith

This is Minnina M. Smith's debut book, "365 Days of Empowerment: Your Daily Dose of Encouragement," I'm thrilled to introduce you to her. With a heartfelt acknowledgment of divine guidance, Minnina draws upon her expertise as a certified life and health coach. From overcoming personal adversities to thriving in a rewarding military career and entrepreneurship, her experiences have shaped her mission: to uplift others on their paths to empowerment. Grounded in unwavering faith, Minnina's book offers personalized support and encouragement, inviting readers to rewrite their narratives and embrace a future filled with purpose and vitality. This is just the beginning of Minnina's journey, with more empowering books to come.

Made in the USA
Middletown, DE
07 February 2025